ASTRO-PICK YOUR PERFECT PARTNER

How to assess accurately and quickly your own special needs in love and sex, and how to rate their compatibility with those of your existing or intended partner.

By the same author
HOW TO ASTRO-ANALYSE YOURSELF AND OTHERS

Astro-Pick Your Perfect Partner

A Step-by-Step Guide to Compatibility in Relationships

by

M. E. COLEMAN B.A., LL.B.

Illustrated by Ellena Clews

THE AQUARIAN PRESS
Wellingborough, Northamptonshire

First published 1986

© M. E. COLEMAN 1986

British Library Cataloguing in Publication Data

Coleman, M. E.
    Astro-pick your perfect partner: a step-by-step
    guide to compatibility in relationships.
    1. Astrology   2. Love
    I. Title
    133.5'83067   BF1729.L6

    ISBN 0-85030-457-1

The Aquarian Press is part of the Thorsons Publishing Group

Printed and bound in Great Britain

CONTENTS

FOREWORD

This is not one more astrology paperback, promising to find you your ideal mate in five easy paragraphs. Neither is it a heavy textbook, filled with complicated graphs, diagrams and formulae that are well nigh incomprehensible to the general reader. Furthermore, this book is not about the kind of astrology represented by newspaper 'Stars' columns, mass-produced magazine 'forecasts' and 'pop' books, which reduce astrology to the level of a foolish fortune-telling device.

Like all other university-qualified psychologists who have also trained themselves in astrological theory and practice, I totally and absolutely reject those varieties of debased, mass-marketed astrology. In the public mind, they serve only to denigrate what has always been a great and beneficient science which could not have survived — largely through the devotion of learned and enquiring minds — for more than three thousand years if all it could do was to tell you, 'Next Tuesday would be a good day to write a letter, have a party or stay at home.'

This book deals with Astro-Analysis and shows you how to use it in deciding compatibility in all types of relationships. The technique itself blends modern psychological methods of personality assessment with precise interpretation of individual birth patterns in the horoscope chart. The technique is not difficult to apply and — if you take the necessary time and trouble — will *never* give you wrong answers.

Easy-to-follow Personality Profile forms and Compatibility Rating Tables are included to ensure no salient point is overlooked. They also teach you 'Synthesis' — the intricate blending together of contrary personality traits and characteristics. In my experience, few textbooks demonstrate this vital (and for beginners, perplexing) process in a manner that can be quickly and fully understood.

Of course, some commentators may assert that I have over-simplified the techniques, since chart factors (which I regard as embellishments) have been discarded. I cannot agree with this view. I have always maintained that if you thoroughly grasp the precise psychological significance of the unique compound of traits, attitudes and drives which the *basic* natal chart reveals, no further 'trimmings' are needed.

The following statement confirms what a good working knowledge of astro-analysis can do for you. It is the latest of many similar comments passed on to me by clients who have successfully used and applied the methods of personality analysis set out in my books.

Two of my clients were told when visiting doctors that 'their understanding of themselves and their relationships was astounding'.

Throughout this book I have consistently sought for clarity in analysis instead of overburdening detail and quality, not quantity, in comment. Once you clearly comprehend the natal chart, it will speak for itself. All you have to do is listen to what it is telling you.

Lastly, I would like to say this to cynics, sceptics and scoffers who 'don't believe in astrology!' Spend as little as one year studying the science through the works of university-qualified authors of which there are many nowadays. Apply what you have learned to your own lives and those around you. Then, let's see what's happened to your opinions.

M. E. Coleman
Sydney, Australia

INTRODUCTION:

Relationships Today . . . Anything Goes — Or Does It?

New Concepts of Love for New Lifestyles

- What makes people fall in *and* out of love?
- Why do an 'impossible couple' create a satisfying marriage, while a 'perfect pair' tear each other apart?
- Does love at first sight *actually* exist?
- And (perhaps the most vital of all) do *you* yourself really want marriage and/or children? Or has someone or something merely pressurized you into thinking you do?

From the beginning of civilization, man has been pursuing the answers to these anguished questions — for thousands of years through the ancient science of astrology and the pairing of the sexes it calls 'synastry', and, more recently, through the thoroughly modern science of psychology and its medical offshoot, psychiatry. For — whether you choose to admit it consciously to yourself or not — the yearning to love and be loved is undoubtedly the most powerful urge in the human psyche. *And* frustration of this urge constitutes a force so destructive that virtually all the physical and psychological ills the flesh is heir to can be laid finally at its door.

This is doubtless why — as the fastest-moving century Planet Earth has ever seen races to its close and the hi-tech world of the next one glitters ever more scarily on the horizon — the same age-old search for love and understanding is going on and the same age-old questions are still being asked. I hear them every day in my own practice as a psychologist/astrologer and in my view, *without* the help of a horoscope chart, they are becoming increasingly tough to answer.

Why is this? Because now is the dawning of the Age of Aquarius and we are being forced to witness the total destruction of the ancient, iron-clad conception of the role of the sexes and a re-definition of the meaning of marriage. Nothing is the way it was. Nothing will ever be the same again. Hence, it is no use looking back to the past to untangle today's problems in love and sexual relationships, which explains why more and more academically trained counsellors are daring to look for the answers in the once-scorned teachings of astrology — despite the scoffing of some colleagues and laymen.

For such cynics, Sir Isaac Newton (the genius physicist who discovered the laws of gravity and revolutionized mathematics) provided the most famous and enduring squelch. When told by a leading astronomer that only fools still believed in astrology, he replied with the calm confidence of the Capricorn he was: 'Sir, I have studied it. You have not.'

In those eight plain words he said everything. With the same eight words, Newton affirmed his faith in the fact that *anyone* who makes a serious and open-minded study of astrology becomes totally unable to scoff. Its truths are inarguable as are the revelations of human personality which appear in an expertly constructed and analysed horoscope chart. (That means, of course, the genuine article, not the mass-produced or computer print-out varieties!)

Probably, the first and greatest modern mind to brush the cobwebs off the science of the stars was the world-famous Swiss psychoanalyst Carl Gustav Jung. Many followed his lead, 'married' the ancient and the modern sciences, and extended his researches. All found that (among much other data) the individual chart offered answers to the conundrums of love or sex which no other form of investigation could.

A complete, minutely detailed portrait of personality which its subject could not fake or distort; and, most significantly, an accurate picture of the manner in which that subject responds to stimuli arousing the emotions, the affections and the passions: put two such astrological personality portraits together, cross-reference them according to the rules of synastry and you have in your hands the key to the compatibility or incompatibility of the pair. This will reveal whether a partnership between them will work easily or painfully — but *not*, mind you, whether they *ought* to marry or not!

Astrology has always adhered to the view (as do most religions) that man is here on earth to learn and evolve. A difficult marriage is one of the toughest ways there is to digest these lessons, yet such a union can teach you much more than a happier one, provided you don't allow yourself to sink into the twin bogs of self-pity and self-recrimination. Obviously, you're going to say a problem marriage is not what you or anybody else *wants*. But astrology maintains that this *may* be just what you need. To understand yourself and the opposite sex better, and to make your personality grow by battling the obstacles and forcing yourself to look for the motes in your own eyes instead of only spotting them in your partner's, you may *need* a difficult marriage.

In compatibility analyses, the roles played by the Sun (basic life attitude and the masculine principle), the Moon (emotional responses and the feminine principle), Venus (the capacity to give and receive love or affection), and Mars (the physical energies and sexuality) are naturally given the closest scrutiny. As you can see, between them the four pinpoint the areas of compatibility or lack of it most likely to show up in any form of permanent union. All four are of paramount importance in the astrology of love and sex and their relationships to each other in the two charts are vital. Mercury (mentality and the ability to express ideas) also needs extra special emphasis in today's world where *communication* has virtually become a sacred word. If a couple cannot or will not communicate with each other, one of them is sure, eventually, to toss in the proverbial towel!

The five planets listed above are thus for obvious reasons tagged as 'personal planets'. The Ascendant (sign rising at the moment of birth) and the other five planets, Jupiter, Saturn, Uranus, Neptune and Pluto, all play their significant roles but in astrological compatibility patterns have lesser overall impact on a relationship.

It should be said now, however (and we'll discuss it at greater length in a later chapter), the Ascendant is always a force to be reckoned with — especially at the outset of a relationship. If it clashes with the Sun or Moon signs, and so masks the true personality of your intended, you may wake up later to discover you've made the horrific mistake of judging a book by its cover. This masking effect is, by the way, the explanation of the old lament: 'That one is a street angel and a house devil.'

Unfortunately, those whose interest in astrology has been only casual rarely realize the intricate interweaving of personality traits and potentials which blend to create a compatible or incompatible pair. This misconception is due to the fact that most 'pop' press features and 'pop' books on astrology shy away from the heavy stuff and stick to the simplicity of the Sun Sign alone, which is what you mean when you call yourself a Leo or a Libra. Most people today know their Sun signs and anyway the twelve are easily and quickly described. Yet, although the Sun sign *is* very important because it reveals the *basic life attitude* of all its natives, it is only one of the larger pieces in the often conflicting mosaic of traits and drives which constitute the *unique* human being that is you.

Regrettably, the popular press's over-emphasis on Sun signs has had some unfortunate results. Many psychologist/astrologers (including myself!) have frequently encountered a worried couple who want to marry but fear, for example, his Aries Sun will clash forever with her Cancer Sun. It will! No doubt about that! The ego thrust of these two signs is resolutely one-pointed *and* aimed in quite different directions. However, the other personal planets in their charts may show a strong, fundamental compatibility. A well-matched approach to love relationships, similar sex drives, harmonious ideas about children and family life. And — further — what do the pair really want and expect of marriage? A life of thunderous confrontations followed by soaked handkerchiefs and passionate reconciliations? Or a peaceful Darby- and-Joan jogtrot together till death do them part? (Their charts can answer those questions too, even if the subjects themselves can't.)

Of course, in the space of a book devoted to the analysis of personal relationships through the science of synastry, the techniques of astrological calculation (i.e. the mathematics required to erect a chart, calculate the precise planetary aspects, the house cusps and Ascendant) cannot be included. However, if you'd like to learn how to erect charts for yourself plus your nearest and/or dearest, you can study such techniques in my companion book, *How to Astro-Analyse Yourself and Others.*

Now, before we move on to watching synastry in action, we had best cast a cool, calm look at what's going on all around us: at the rapidly changing world we're hoping to find our private dreams of fulfilment in; at the totally new concepts of love and lifestyles now emerging; at the reasons why the whole relationship picture is suddenly acquiring a startlingly different perspective.

The Aquarian Age Love Scene

No use glumly wondering where love has gone, or complaining that everybody chats up everybody else but nobody *cares*, or keeping a stiff upper lip as yet another relationship sinks without a trace, or cursing the fact that women have inexplicably begun to think like men. We've got to get to grips with the force behind the changes if we're going to come out on top of them. And *that* means taking a trip, way, way back in time to a starry night in March 1781 when an expatriate German choirmaster trained his home-made telescope on the London skies and discovered the cause of it all!

The choirmaster's name was Frederich Herschel. His discovery's name was Uranus, the progenitor of the Aquarian Age. A planet whose erratic, iconoclastic force is symbolized by a bolt of jagged blue lightning and whose escalating impact on mass consciousness as the world moves forward into the last decades of the twentieth century is the astrological explanation of drastic, swift and irreversible changes in human relationships.

Also known as the Great Disruptor, Uranus' whole task is to break up the crystallized patterns of living in a lightning-type flash — forcing us to change (whether we like it or not!), jolting us out of our comfortable little ruts, compelling us to look at life and love in a totally new, even disconcerting manner. So if we aim to handle our relationships successfully while the cold, bright dawning of the Age of Aquarius lights up the horizon, we need to become better acquainted with Uranus himself and the sign he rules — which, of course, requires a brief look at the ancient myths surrounding the god after which Aquarius' ruler was named.

Uranus, according to Greek mythology, was the husband of the Great Earth-Mother. Between them they produced a fearsome collection of offspring, one of whom was named Saturn. But Uranus was so disgusted with the appearance of the bunch that he thrust the lot down into the deepest abyss for ever.

However, his wife, like Queen Victoria, was not amused. She wanted her family back, blood-curdling as they were, and rescued the only one tough enough to tackle his formidable father. This was Saturn. And even at the beginning of time, Saturn proved himself to be as implacable as ever. He caught Uranus unawares, chopped him to pieces and hurled the bits to the four winds of the world.

In the case of anyone but a god, that would have been most definitely that! But gods have a way of coping and Uranus did. Nevertheless, as you'll agree after digesting the foregoing tale of treachery, patricide, wifely dirty-dealing, etc., Uranus was left with a distinctly jaundiced view of family life. He *had* tried it once. And he didn't like it! Which is why — in each individual horoscope as well as in mass changes — the planet Uranus represents severance of ties, dislike of permanent commitment, sudden break-ups in the routine of living, distaste for all that is soft, yielding or sentimental — the 'I'll-go-my-way-and-to-hell-with-everyone' attitude.

Those reactions sound familiar, don't they? And so do the plaintive cries psychologists, psychiatrists and astrologers hear on every hand . . . 'Where am I going? What's happening to my relationships? Why doesn't anyone care anymore?' With Uranus at the wheel, the answers to those questions are disquieting, to say the least, especially if you like your world to be calm, predictable and secure.

Wherever you *thought* you were going, you're sure to end up someplace else. Whatever you hoped for in your relationships, you're likely to get the opposite. And if you feel nobody cares about you, a spot of quiet introspection might reveal that you don't care about them! Shocking? Perverse? Bizarre? True. But Uranus loves to shock, is most definitely not in the 'romantic dream' business, and reckons if you haven't yet learned to be fiercely independent, it's about time you did. So as Uranus is a lot bigger than all of us on Planet Earth, we might as well play along. Which means we've got to accept that from here on in *change is the name of the game*. We must become as flexible as bamboos in a hurricane and ride out the whirlwinds.

For those with a strong Aquarian flavour in their natal charts, it's likely to be a trifle easier. Equally for those who have Uranus powerfully placed. Such individuals are basically rather better tuned in to the idea of endless upheavals, new starts, flying off at tangents, tangling with technology, flashing insights into the shape of things to come. So, let's see now what we can learn from them in coping with Uranus and the Age of Aquarius in the form of quotes I've collected from clients in the above categories, who've discussed their feelings with me. Remember that the following individuals have the sign of Aquarius and/or the planet Uranus dominating their charts. To those with a more traditional and conventional viewpoint, these comments may sound harsh, unsentimental, even weird, but both Uranus and his sign do exhibit all those traits plus an oddly impersonal concept of love and sex.

Case No. 1 raises the question . . . Will the Aquarian Age turn the act of love merely into an act of friendship? This male remarked that, although he'd remarried, he often slept with his ex-wife because he knew she still loved him. 'It's the least I can do for her!' said he.

Case No. 2 raises the question . . . Will the Aquarian Age offer the reincarnation theory as the explanation of habitual non-commitment? This female remarked that she had no desire for permanency in relationships as she'd done all that in previous existences. 'I find all the men I go to bed with are just past-lives' experiences. Ancient history!'

Case No. 3 raises the question . . . Will the Aquarian Age create a completely new scenario for marriage? This male remarked that he organized a large family wedding in the time-honoured style but wrote and performed the ceremony himself. This meant, of course, the marriage had no legal validity. 'I had to do something different!' said he.

Case No. 4 raises the question . . . Will the Aquarian Age redefine the meaning of commitment? This female remarked that, after pursuing her concept of marital bliss through three fruitless trips to the altar, she'd decided to make her expectations clearer to her next man. 'No ties! No promises! No everlasting vows this time! I want someone to share my freedom!'

Well, there's the Aquarian Age banner for you . . . waving brightly in the breeze.

The whirlwinds of change are everywhere. Uprooting all the old, tried-and-true values in love and sex. Tearing down tradition in family life. Rushing us to the brink of what writer Aldous Huxley once called the 'Brave New World'. But, personally, I don't think it will be as terrifying as the prophets of doom and the prevailing mood of pessimism they engender may imply. The secret of relating in the current scene is mainly a matter of reminding ourselves that after 2,000 years the Piscean Age — with all its Neptune-inspired fantasies, illusions and romanticized dreams is over.

Thus we must not look back with nostalgic yearning to what *was*. We must look ahead to what *will be*. Neither Uranus nor Aquarians waste time sugar-coating the pill of truth and both will help if we're prepared to tackle the future by pursuing the twin ideals of self-honesty and self-awareness.

As the nineteenth-century poet Tennyson once wrote:

> The old order changeth, yielding place to new
> And God fulfils Himself in many ways . . .

Or, to go back to the beginning of this section and put it another way — maybe love hasn't gone at all but we're being compelled to look at it in an entirely new way. Maybe caring about others is taking new forms too. Less personal but far more global. People care about the fate of the earth and its environment, about inequality and injustice in a way they never did before. Maybe the fact that women do think now more like men will end the battle of the sexes and create equal partnership instead of subjugation.

In her lengthy book, *Astrology: A Cosmic Science*, author Isabel Hickey once mentioned that most of us live by the old saying, 'Better the devil you know, than the devil you don't. But,' said she, 'why do we assume the devil you don't know *is* a devil? He *could* turn out to be an angel in disguise!'

That, in my view, is the best way of handling the onrush of the Aquarian Age. Look beneath the chaos and confusion, flow with the tide of progress and you'll discover there still is a pot of gold at the end of the Uranian rainbow.

Now, let's get ready to put synastry to work and discover who's likely to fall for who and why. Of course, love itself cannot be neatly defined and continues to defy the attempts of the world's greatest thinkers. There are so many kinds of love. So many ways in which it tries to reveal itself. One man's meat is another man's poison. One woman's seventh heaven is another's private hell. But we can begin to gain a clearer picture of what you and your love partner expect from relationships by examining what I'll call 'Elemental Attractions'.

CHAPTER ONE

Elemental Attractions . . . A Switch-On or Switch-Off?

The Four Elements: Their role in Attraction or Dislike

> Love just happens . . . and who knows why?
> We can't pick and choose the one.
> A glance, a touch, a certain smile —
> That's all and the thing is done —
> For ever and ever . . . for people like me

That short quotation from an old song pinpoints the yearning and help-lessness we feel when real love pierces the heart but the loved person turns away and we are alone again. But why did love happen in the first place? Why does it last for ever and ever for some of us and vanish in a flash for others? Did we in fact choose the wrong person to love, or did we merely make some foolish mistake in the manner we behaved towards him/her? Synastry can point the way to solving the eternal riddles of love and sexual attraction because it allows us to look behind the social mask and discover the true self, in a manner that does not permit delusion or fantasy.

Certainly some individuals are much inclined to fall in love at first sight. Others meet someone who appeals and patiently wait for the relationship to grow. Yet in both situations, the reason you even look twice at the stranger across the crowded room has its basis in what I term 'elemental attractions'.

When you feel as if you're 'in your element', you are in fact instinctively responding to compatible elemental patterns in your own horoscope chart and those close to you, because each of the twelve signs of the zodiac is linked to one of the four elements: fire, air, earth and water.

But for readers who are not fully familiar with their specific chart patterns, I must point out that the element you'll feel most comfortable with is not necessarily the element of your Sun sign.

The true elemental picture only emerges when both charts have been erected and the elements affecting all ten planets, i.e. Sun, Moon, Mercury, Venus, Mars, Jupiter, Saturn, Uranus, Neptune and Pluto, plus Ascendant and Midheaven, have been checked. This will show at a glance if you and your partner are strongly fire, air, earth or water personality types. And, as we'll discover in the following pages, attraction or the reverse of it usually begin at elemental levels, representing the foundation of compatibility or incompatibility. (This applies to our everyday family relationships as well as those with lovers.)

To illustrate: A strongly fire personality type often experiences great difficulty in breaking free of early parental conditioning if the first home scene involved earth-type parents. As one of my clients put it: 'I always felt claustrophobic in my parents' presence. Their heavy, earthy approach to life constantly smothered my enthusiasm. Sort of — put out my fire!' Yet, because she had been subconsciously conditioned to live in an earthy environment, she sought out an earth-type partner in adult life and therefore repeated the whole grim story.

Thus are the sins of the parents visited on the children! For what we learnt at mother's knee or on father's lap dictates our adult decisions to a far higher degree than most of us realize. (More about this in Chapter 2.)

To take a light example of elemental group reactions, I remember a peaceful picnic party of about eight people. Everyone was either a strongly earth or water type so we sat about quietly and comfortably communicating. Enter a double Gemini with a powerful air stress in her chart and the whole show fell apart in minutes. Nobody could cope with that sudden, hassling inrush of air!

I think it's easier to understand the elemental picture if you bear in mind that astrology is basically a language of symbols. Think of the four elements — as they are in nature — and you'll immediately gain a better impression of how they affect human personality. Think of the crackling brightness of a fire; the deep currents of the sea; the rushing winds of air; the rocklike solidity of earth. Then apply your image to the twelve signs. Predominantly fire types *are* bright, warm, crackling with energy; predominantly water types *are* deep, reflective, responding to the currents of their moods; predominantly air types *are* light, blowing hither and thither, flying off to the intellectual stratosphere; predominantly earth types *are* solid, unchanging as the seasons, tilling the often hard soil of life.

To take our elemental symbolism a step further: fire and air on the one hand are elements with a natural affinity. Both are intangible in the sense that neither can be held in your hand. Thus individuals with strong fire patterns usually get along more easily with others who have strong air patterns. The entire confrontation is light, bright, quick, flashing. But it can be overly volatile, even explosive. Fire is capable of burning up air's oxygen: air is just as capable of blowing out a fire as it is of fanning the flames. Hence a union between a fire type and an air type can be exciting but short-lived.

The same comparison applies to earth and water, again elements with a natural affinity. Thus individuals (as quoted in the foregoing little anecdote) with strong earth patterns usually feel at ease in the presence of those with strong water patterns. The exchange is solid, deep, calm, refreshing. But it can be overly heavy, almost soggy. Earth's dryness can block the flow of water's currents; water can just as easily turn earth into a quagmire as it can nourish it.

So, if you're feeling hassled, drowned, smothered or burnt up in your current lifestyle, look to the elemental patterns of those around you in your public or private environments. If you're not 'in your element', maybe, it's time you changed it! Or, failing the more drastic remedy, you'll be able to cope much better with alien elemental attitudes around you when you better understand their needs.

Battling the Elements . . . Yours and Your Partner's

With the relevant charts in hand, note down which planets are in which of the twelve signs on a sheet of paper. (Later in this book, we'll see how to prepare and use a Compatibility Rating Table, but for now we'll stick mainly to contrasting elemental pictures.) Next, read the analyses that apply to each of your listed personal planets, i.e. Sun, Moon, Mercury, Venus and Mars. You'll be surprised at how your insight into motivation (yours *and* your partner's) is deepened even at this very early stage in your understanding of synastry.

This check is equally helpful with people in your life less significant than a love partner. The boss, friends, relatives, for example. And for this quick check-up, you won't need to erect a complete chart for them. All you require is their birth-date and country of birth. Simply write down from the appropriate ephemeris (Planetary Tables) the signs their personal planets occupy and examine the elemental pattern which emerges.

You'll quickly see why the boss flies off the handle in a split-second when there's trouble at home. Or why your favourite uncle invariably buys birthday presents you don't much fancy. Incidentally, I mention 'country of birth' in the preceding paragraph because of the Moon's swift motion. Should the Moon be close to a cusp (i.e. borderline between two signs) your chosen subject's birthplace can mean the Moon actually occupies the *next* sign to that shown in the ephemeris. Or, especially in the case of subjects born in the Southern Hemisphere, the Moon may occupy the sign *before* that shown in the ephemeris. If the Moon is near a cusp, it is safest to consider in any event the influence of both the signs concerned.

Take care, of course, to check the planetary tables carefully. Don't get mixed up and think because you have Venus in Aries, you'll have Mars there too.

Some charts, like my own, do have three of the personal planets all clustered cosily together in the same sign — which fact lets that sign run the whole show, hog the spotlight and bore everyone to death with the predictability of its response. Much more often, thank heaven, these planets are better spread around the signs, thus producing greater variety of reaction and added 'spice' in the total personality. The following will serve to illustrate.

Your chosen subject might have Sun in Sagittarius, Moon in Aquarius, Mercury in Capricorn, Venus in Scorpio and Mars in Leo. A tantalizing mixed bag of contrary responses if ever there was one! With a blend of fiery ego thrust, airily detached emotions, earthy hard-headed thinking, engulfing waves of water-type affection and fiery, dramatically displayed sexuality. Life will never be a trip through a rose garden with this mix — for its owner or anyone else that tangles with him/her.

Predominant Elements in Your Charts

As noted earlier in this chapter, most individuals can be loosely classified into fire types, earth types, air types, and water types. We arrive at such classification by merely adding up the elemental emphasis on the date and year of birth from the planetary positions in the appropriate ephemeris.

For beginners, here's a spot-check of the signs in their elemental groupings. (You'll observe these are also included with the complete analyses of the behavioural responses applying to each of the twelve which follow.)

FIRE signs: Aries, Leo, Sagittarius
AIR signs: Gemini, Libra, Aquarius
EARTH signs: Taurus, Virgo, Capricorn
WATER signs: Cancer, Scorpio, Pisces

Remember, when thousands of years ago, the ancients first assigned an element to each sign, they didn't do this at random:

Fire was given to Aries, Leo and Sagittarius because these signs do exhibit ardour, keenness, activity and enthusiasm in their various modes within human personality . . . the burning, leaping brightness of the element of fire itself.

Air was given to Gemini, Libra and Aquarius because these signs do exhibit intellectuality, communicativeness and lightness in their various modes within human personality . . . the intangible, rushing winds of the element of air itself.

Earth was given to Taurus, Virgo and Capricorn because these signs do exhibit practicality, caution and stability in their various modes within human personality . . . the solid, unyielding support of the element of earth itself.

Water was given to Cancer, Scorpio and Pisces because these signs do exhibit fluidity, sensitivity and depths in their various modes within human personality . . . the flowing, reflective unfathomability of the element of water itself.

Now, take a look at your partner's chart and your own (if you have these) or total up the elemental stress patterns from the ephemeris. Use all ten planets for this — Jupiter, Saturn, Uranus, Neptune and Pluto, as well as the five personal planets. Add an extra point each for the Sun and Moon, and another point each for the Ascendant and Midheaven if you have these calculated.

Your results will list like this example — taken from a 1940s ephemeris for June 1945:

Subject: Female born at 5.45 a.m. in Sydney, Australia on 16.6.45

Fire signs:	1 planet (Pluto in Fire.)	Total = 1 point.
Air signs:	4 planets + extra point for Sun and Ascendant. (Sun, Mercury, Uranus, Neptune + Ascendant in Air)	
		Total = 6 points
Earth signs:	4 planets + extra point for Moon. (Moon, Venus, Jupiter and Mars in Earth)	
		Total = 5 points.
Water signs:	1 planet + Midheaven. (Saturn and Midheaven in Water)	Total = 2 points.

Now you can see at a glance this subject is a predominantly air type, but much more practical than would otherwise be the case because earth is also strongly stressed. Neither really passionate nor spontaneous, a very low fire score. Basically unemotional . . . very low water score.

To summarize and generalize:
Predominantly *fire* types tend to regard love and sexual adventures basically as *exciting activities,* to be dashed into enthusiastically and instantly as the fancy takes them.

Predominantly *air* types tend to regard love and sexual adventures basically as *interesting exchanges,* to be flown into lightly but in the hope of intellectual as well as physical entertainment.

Predominantly *earth* types tend to regard love and sexual adventures as basically *high-priority tasks,* to be handled competently and calmly with due attention to detail.

Predominantly *water* types tend to regard love and sexual adventures as basically *intense experiences,* to be floated into warily but in the hope of sinking peacefully at last into a pool of mutual devotion.

The Polarities and Quadruplicities

When you turn to whichever of the 12 signs you're working with, you'll observe that each is slotted into two further sub-groupings, technically known as the Polarities and the Quadruplicities. These two sub-groupings offer further valuable keys to anticipating the characteristic mode of operation of each personality. And more importantly, as we'll discuss in a later chapter, whether they create ease or tension in a single natal chart or when two potential partner's charts are compared.

A. Polarities Sub-group

Herein signs are divided into positive or negative categories. All the fire and air signs are tagged 'Positive', all earth and water signs are tagged 'Negative'. These adjectives do not have the same meaning as they do in common speech.

Positive signs predispose towards self-expressive, positive and extroverted behaviour.

Negative signs predispose towards self-repressive, receptive and introverted behaviour.

When dealing with sub-group A, remember that a heavy score in Positive signs in a female chart does not mean the subject is a bulldozer. It does mean she is pretty direct and not much sold on traditional female wiles. The same applies vice versa in the male chart. A heavy score of negative signs does not mean he is a door-mat. It does mean he takes a more indirect approach and is more likely to circumnavigate a problem than meet it head on.

B. Quadruplicities Sub-group

Herein signs are divided into cardinal, fixed or mutable categories. Aries, Cancer, Libra and Capricorn are tagged 'Cardinal'. Taurus, Leo, Scorpio and Aquarius are tagged 'Fixed'. Gemini, Virgo, Sagittarius and Pisces are tagged 'Mutable'.

Cardinal signs indicate innate qualities of enterprise, initiative and thrust.

Fixed signs indicate innate qualities of steadfastness, stability and determination.

Mutable signs indicate innate qualities of adaptability, versatility and willingness to work with others.

When dealing with sub-group B, remember none of the cardinal signs get on really comfortably with each other. Too much egocentricity, too much relentless push towards differing goals. Again, the same applies to the fixed and mutable groups. The fixed signs find each other too stubborn, too inflexible. The mutable signs are lost in each other's company, confused by this reflection of their own changeability.

Now, we've worked our way through the elements, the polarities and the quadruplicities, we'll start to put human personality under the microscope with individual sign and planetary interpretation in twelve easy-to-follow segments.

Quick reference check-points

Elements: Fire = Aries, Leo & Sagittarius.
          Air   = Gemini, Libra & Aquarius.
          Earth = Taurus, Virgo, Capricorn.
          Water = Cancer, Scorpio & Pisces.
          (In some texts, the elemental grouping is called
          'The Triplicities'.)

Polarities: Positive = Aries, Gemini, Leo, Libra, Sagittarius &
                      Aquarius.
          Negative = Taurus, Cancer, Virgo, Scorpio,
                      Capricorn & Pisces.

Quadruplicities: Cardinal = Aries, Cancer, Libra & Capricorn.
               Fixed   = Taurus, Leo, Scorpio & Aquarius.
               Mutable = Gemini, Virgo, Sagittarius & Pisces.

Compatibility — Yes or No? The Sign and Planet Picture

This is where we begin to discover what really is 'going on behind your eyes' . . . your own and your love partner's. This is where we begin to assemble the multi-faceted patterns of personality and place them together like the pieces of an intriguing jigsaw puzzle.

In each of the twelve segments, you'll see we've spotlighted the elemental background of the signs by using terms which call up the right image, e.g. fiery images for fire-type behaviour. But it will extend your insight further if you also visualize as clearly as possible the animal or mythological figure, representing any one of the twelve. You're handling

Aries planets? Call up a vivid mental image of a real ram. You're thinking about Libra? Imagine a set of finely balanced scales. (By the way, complete visualization for the signs of the zodiac are set out in detail in my companion book, *How to Astro-Analyze Yourself and Others.*)

To make the best use of the individual sign interpretations, check through your prepared list of planetary positions for yourself and partner. Then select which particular paragraph of interpretation for both sign and planet applies. Mark each one for future reference.

At this stage, we've omitted a consideration of the Ascendant and Mercury as each of these receives separate assessment later in this book.

No. 1.   The Fire Sign of Aries
Symbol: the Charging figure of the Ram.
Behavioural keyword: 'I am!'
Classification: Positive cardinal.

Sun in Aries = Basic life attitude. Fundamental approach to living is self-assertive, brash, extroverted, enterprising and independent. Adventure, excitement and up-and-at'em activity turn this type on. If unrestrained by other planets in the natal chart, the attendant egotism, rashness and lack of consideration turn others off.

Moon in Aries = Basic emotional attitude. Emotional reactions are instantaneous, eager and forceful. Feelings erupt like a volcano and just as suddenly cool down. To some, these fireworks are exciting, enticing. To others, the display is much too pushy, too overwhelming, too unthinking.

Venus in Aries = Basic love nature. Reponses to love and affection are forceful, warm and flatteringly keen. Love is all and all is love *while* the moment lasts. But later some recipients may realize that Aries fire can burn as well as warm the heart.

Mars in Aries = Basic sex nature. Physical energies and passions blaze like an out-of-control bushfire. The velocity of this sex drive is breathtaking, the taste for violent and sudden love affairs virtually insatiable, the heedlessness incredible. The other stop-at-nothing lovers of the zodiac can cope. Gentler spirits shrivel up before it.

Love Lines for Love Signs

No. 1. Aries . . . the Ram personality Type Female

Here's how SHE feels about love. SHE's into instant action.

'We lay beneath the willow tree.
'The moonlight made us dapple.
'He offered me a red, red rose,
'I countered with an apple.

'Our kiss burnt centuries away,
'We heard The Serpent's laughter:
'So once was Eden lost, they say . . .
'But DAMN the morning after!'

No. 2   The Earth Sign of Taurus
Symbol: the Stalwart figure of the Bull.
Behavioural keyword: 'I have!'
Classification: Negative fixed.

Sun in Taurus = Basic life attitude. Fundamental approach to living is self-repressive, patient, introverted, constructive and team-oriented. Solid achievement, physical plus financial ease, and reliable performance turn this type on. If unrestrained by other planets in the natal chart, the attendant acquisitiveness, inflexibility and possessiveness turn others off.

Moon in Taurus = Basic emotional attitude. Emotional reactions are deep, long-lasting and controlled. Feelings grow as slowly as seeds and are not quick to show themselves. To some, such solid earthiness is intensely reassuring. To others, the result is much too heavy, too lacking in spontaneity, too persevering.

Venus in Taurus = Basic love nature. Response to love and affection are markedly physical, sensual and reliable. The capacity for love is as deep and enveloping as the earth itself. But later some recipients may find the sheer weight of Taurus affection too ponderous to bear.

Mars in Taurus = Basic sex nature. Physical energies and passions echo the same consistent, persistent constancy and repeat it for ever and ever. The sex drive is slow to rouse but once awakened nothing short of an earthquake will stop it. Linked with it is an equally passionate urge for physical and financial security. The other long-distance performers of the zodiac can cope. Lighter spirits flee.

Love Lines for Love Signs

No. 2. Taurus . . . the Bull personality Type Male

Here's how HE feels about love. HE's into solid results.

'I like your eyes. I like your lips.
'I like those curved 'Earth Mother' hips.
'I'd like to pace you running free
'Across the Hills of Home with me.

'But while I write you in my book . . .
'The clincher question: CAN you cook?'

No. 3   The Air Sign of Gemini
Symbol: the Double-Bodied figure of the Twins.
Behavioural keyword; 'I think!'
Classification: Positive mutable.

Sun in Gemini = *Basic life attitude.* Fundamental approach to living is self-expressive, intelligent, extroverted, multi-faceted and entertaining. Ingenuity, intellectual challenges, clever conversational exchanges turn this type on. If unrestrained by other planets in the natal map, the attendant superficiality, lack of continuity and two-facedness turn others off.

Moon in Gemini = *Basic emotional attitude.* Emotional reactions are light-hearted, cool and startlingly versatile. Feelings flit like butterflies and are just about as hard to catch. To some, all the colour and brightness is irresistible. To others, the display is much too hollow, too unemotional, too fickle.

Venus in Gemini = *Basic love nature.* Responses to love and affection are charming, fluent and airily sophisticated. Flirtation is always the favourite game in the executive suite and any number can play. But later some participants may realize neither quick wit nor quicker quips speak the language of the heart.

Mars in Gemini = *Basic sex nature.* Physical energies and passions are equally light, lively but seldom long-lasting. The sex drive diffuses itself like thistledown, blowing this way and that in the search for cleverer partners and more amusing liaisons. The other intellectual lovers of the zodiac can cope. Sterner spirits recoil.

Love Lines for Love Signs

No. 3. Gemini . . . the Twins personality Type Female

Here's how SHE feels about love. SHE's into flirting and flitting.

'Some men I like.
'Some men I don't.
'Some because they love me . . .
'Some because they WON'T!'

No. 4   The Water Sign of Cancer
Symbol: the Hard-Shelled figure of the Crab.
Behavioural keyword: 'I feel!'
Classification: Negative cardinal.

Sun in Cancer = Basic life attitude. Fundamental approach to living is self-repressive, intuitive, introverted, home-oriented and considerate. Resourcefulness, tenacity in pursuit of goals and the simple, domestic joys turn this type on. If unrestrained by other planets in the natal map, the attendant touchiness, self-pity and hypersensitivity turn others off.

Moon in Cancer = Basic emotional attitude. Emotional reactions are clingingly romantic, rather damply sentimental and naturally self-sacrificing. Feelings well up like a tidal wave from the depths, sweeping all before them. To some, the sight of such a wall of watery intensity is wondrously satisfying. To others, the display is too undisciplined, too suffocating, too wet.

Venus in Cancer = Basic love nature. Responses to love and affection are tender, cherishing and protective. The heart is always worn prominently on the sleeve with the words 'God Bless Our Home' emblazoned beneath it. But later some recipients may realize such unreasoning devotion is as heavy to handle as a bucket of water.

Mars in Cancer = Basic Sex Nature. Physical energies and passions are similarly weighty and just as likely to spill over without apparent provocation. The powerful sex drive often creates strife in expressing itself because the will has become dependent on the mood of the moment. The other intuitive lovers of the zodiac can cope. More spontaneous spirits swim for cover.

Love Lines for Love Signs

No. 4. Cancer . . . the Crab personality Type Male

Here's how HE feels about love. HE's into jumping off the deep end.

'My love is like the boundless sea,
'As drenching, deep and ornery.
'Towering as a tidal wave,
'Precious as a pearl-strewn cave.
'Full of current, rock and rip
'To sink you like a floundering ship . . .
'So if that daunts you, little pet —
'Best NOT to get your swimsuit wet.'

No. 5   The Fire Sign of Leo
Symbol: the Lordly figure of the Lion.
Behavioural keyword: 'I will!'
Classification: Positive fixed.

Sun in Leo = Basic life attitude. Fundamental approach to living is self-expressive, power-oriented, extroverted, proud and commanding. Opportunities for leadership, broadmindedness and doing everything 'the big way' turn this type on. If unrestrained by other planets in the natal map, the attendant arrogance, intolerance and pomposity turn others off.

Moon in Leo = Basic emotional attitude. Emotional reactions are powerful, sincere and usually delivered at full blast. Feelings are waved like a banner and always presented centre stage. To some, the no-expense-spared extravaganza is endlessly entertaining. To others, the display is too overdone, too ridiculous, too patronizing.

Venus in Leo = Basic love nature. Responses to love and affection are lavish, open-hearted and almost childishly trusting. The urge to spread sunshine through the adored one's life is heartfelt and genuine. But later some recipients may realize that in return lifelong homage and admiration are also decreed.

Mars in Leo = Basic sex nature. Physical energies and passions are equally hefty, dynamic and filled with a lusty animal appetite for life. The sex drive is all 'heart' but liberally and constantly fuelled by an indomitable will. The other lusty lovers of the zodiac can cope. Less energetic spirits are scorched.

Love Lines for Love Signs

No. 5. Leo . . . the Lion personality Type Male

Here's how HE feels about love. HE's into extravaganzas.

'O, Lady, Lady listen PLEASE
'While swatting up the mysteries
'Of potions, charms and sexpertise
'To help you get your man.

'If you're NOT my kind of mate —
'I.e. spunky, warm and simply great,
'There's NOTHING short of poisoned bait —
'So catch me IF you can!'

No. 6.   The Earth Sign of Virgo
Symbol: the White-Robed figure of the Virgin.
Behavioural keyword: 'I analyse!'
Classification: Negative mutable.

Sun in Virgo = Basic life attitude. Fundamental approach to living is self-effacing, work-oriented, introverted, prudent and practical. Facts, discrimination and well-ordered, detailed minds turn this type on. If unrestrained by other planets in the natal chart, the attendant pedantry, faddiness and overdone modesty turn others off.

Moon in Virgo = Basic emotional attitude. Emotional reactions are conventional, refined and dutifully shown as protocol requires. Feelings are firmly restrained and glimpsed rather than seen — like a face behind lace curtains. To some, such impenetrable decorum is provocative. To others, the display is too studied, too inhibited, too prudish.

Venus in Virgo = Basic love nature. Responses to love and affection are cool, appraising and thoughtful. Practical considerations get mixed up with the hearts and flowers material to the point that everyone wilts before anyone surrenders. But later some recipients may decide a unanimous 'Yes' vote *was* worth waiting for.

Mars in Virgo = Basic sex nature. Physical energies and passions are likewise kept in check like a troupe of well-trained but extremely ferocious animals. The sex drive is thus surprisingly strong and pursues its satisfaction with relentless and applied determination. The other practical lovers of the zodiac can cope. Less earnest spirits retreat.

Love Lines for Love Signs

No. 6. Virgo . . . the Virgin personality Type Male

Here's how HE feels about love. HE's into sensible sensuality.

'In the course of evolution
'I fear we've met with retribution
'For becoming so superior to our kind.
'And while less mental types of fauna
'Live it up in every corner
'We are wrestling with the riddles of the mind.

'Even in the mating season,
'For which there's rarely rhyme or reason,
'We gravitate up to the highest plains.
'Which just of late has made me wonder
'If it wasn't all a blunder
'To evolve ourselves an overload of brains!'

No. 7   The Air Sign of Libra
Symbol: the Balancing figure of the scales.
Behavioural keyword: 'I balance!'
Classification: Positive cardinal.

Sun in Libra = *Basic life attitude.* Fundamental approach to living is pleasant, companionable, extroverted, people-oriented and diplomatic. Impartial argument, harmonious environments and elegance in appearance and action turn this type on. If unrestrained by other planets in the natal map, the attendant shallowness, indecision and fence-sitting turn others off.

Moon in Libra = *Basic emotional attitude.* Emotional reactions are easy-going, gracious and custom-built to maintain peace at virtually any price. Feelings emerge as smoothly and neatly as a computer print-out and are just as intelligently arranged. To some, such idealized presentation assures friction-free encounters. To others, the display is too contrived, too mechanical, too uncommitted.

Venus in Libra = *Basic love nature.* Responses to love and affection are curiously naïve, always refined and unobtrusively charming. Union is the aim of the game yet it is predominantly one of the intellect, not of the body. Later some recipients may decide that love is more than a matter of appealing gestures or pretty words and can never be weighed in the scales of the mind.

Mars in Libra = Basic sex nature. Physical energies and passions also hang forever in the balance, tipping this way and that in the ceaseless pursuit of perfect unity with a perfect mate. The sex drive is thus urgent, hungry for satisfaction yet too often affronted by the stark reality of the act itself. The other elegant lovers of the zodiac can cope. Less idealistic spirits turn away.

Love Lines for Love Signs

No. 7. Libra . . . the Scales personality Type Female

Here's how SHE feels about love. SHE's into elegant amours.

'What, marry YOU? Well, I don't know.
'We'll have to weigh each con and pro.
'You've got a mind . . . I'll grant you that.
'But MUST you wear a TOWELLING
hat?

'I dig your shoulders, hips and waist . . .
'But why this prehistoric haste
'To wed me? . . . OR . . . DID you say
'Bed me?'

No. 8   The Water Sign of Scorpio
Symbol: the Indomitable figure of the Scorpion.
Behavioural keyword: 'I desire!'
Classification: Negative fixed.

Sun in Scorpio = *Basic life attitude.* Fundamental approach to living is intense, purposeful, introverted, success-oriented and tough. Penetrating perception, subtle manoeuvring and no-holds-barred confrontations turn this type on. If unrestrained by other planets in the natal map, the attendant jealousy, unsubstantiated suspicion and stubborn steering along collision courses turn others off.

Moon in Scorpio = *Basic emotional attitude.* Emotional reactions are heavy, powerfully felt and brooded over in secret. Feelings are pent up until they burst out in a torrent of such depth and magnitude, it has to be experienced to be believed. To some, the sheer drama of Scorpio emotion is magnificently inspiring. To others, the display is too overpowering, too disproportionate, too consuming.

Venus in Scorpio = *Basic love nature.* Responses to love and affection are reckless, highly charged and directed towards absolute conquest. In love, as in war, there are no compromises, no second thoughts, no frivolities. But later some recipients may discover they have lost not only their hearts but themselves as well.

Mars in Scorpio = *Basic sex nature.* Physical energies and passions, once they break the banks of iron self-control, rush outwards like a river in flood, tearing down obstacles, opposition and anything else which stands in their path. The sex drive is thus massive, voraciously sensual and permits nothing to thwart it for long. Nor does it forget or forgive infidelities. The other impassioned lovers of the zodiac can cope. Less single-minded spirits run for their lives.

Love Lines for Love Signs

No. 8. Scorpio . . . the Scorpion personality Type Female

Here's how SHE feels about love. SHE's into total conquests.

'Stolen fruit?
'Sweeter than what's rightful.
'Stolen kiss?
'So much more delightful.
'LITTLE girls the single apples please.
'I find *I* want to steal the trees!'

No. 9   The Fire Sign of Sagittarius
Symbol: the Arrow-Aiming figure of the Centaur.
Behavioural Keyword: 'I see!'
Classification: Positive mutable.

Sun in Sagittarius = Basic life attitude. Fundamental approach to living is hearty, hopeful, extroverted, travel-oriented and philosophical. Straight-from-the-shoulder talk, sincerity and adventurous sorties into new worlds in both the physical *and* mental sense turn this type on. If unrestrained by other planets in the natal map, the attendant tactlessness, moralizing and disdain for finnicky detail turn others off.

Moon in Sagittarius = Basic emotional attitude. Emotional reactions are genial, impatient and motivated by the wish for thrill-a-minute experiences. Feelings burn more cheerily than a bonfire on a cold night but often burn down as swiftly. To some, such all-pervading warmth is infallibly comforting. To others, the display is too open, too all-embracing, too brief.

Venus in Sagittarius = Basic love nature. Responses to love and affection are honest, breezy and notably democratic. The accent is far more on being a great pal than a great lover and heart-to-heart confrontations are nimbly avoided. As a result, there are never any attempts to dictate, dominate or restrain. But later some recipients may decide that to Sagittarius freedom and fickleness are easily interchangeable words.

Mars in Sagittarius = Basic sex nature. Physical energies and passions are similarly wayward, wandering and cannot be permanently harnessed to any one person or one place. There is always another escapade, another adventure over the greener hills or round the next corner. The sex drive is thus hearty but applies itself more to athletics than histrionics in achieving satisfaction — often with a casual unconcern for the hour or the location. The other physical lovers of the zodiac can cope. More romantic spirits despair.

Clews

Love Lines for Love Signs

No. 9. Sagittarius . . . the Centaur personality Type Female

Here's how SHE feels about love. SHE's into physical pair-offs.

> 'The partner I like most to meet
> 'Is the husky ATH-L-ETE.
> 'The guy whose conversation ranges
> 'From football scores to cricket changes.

> 'He skis and scubas, surfs and glides,
> 'Strikes terror in opposing sides,
> 'So with this male of mega muscle . . .
> 'Who cares if love's a sort of tussle!'

No. 10   The Earth Sign of Capricorn
Symbol: the High-Climbing figure of the Mountain Goat.
Behavioural keyword: 'I use!'
Classification: Negative cardinal.

Sun in Capricorn = Basic life attitude. Fundamental approach to living is provident, businesslike, introverted, prestige-oriented and practical. Resourcefulness, self-discipline and punctilious obedience to the call of duty turn this type on. If unrestrained by other planets in the natal map, the attendant severity, conservatism and lack of spontaneity turn others off.

Moon in Capricorn = Basic emotional attitude. Emotional reactions are calm, controlled and designed to establish workable relationships. Feelings are never allowed to run riot and willingly accept the correct, the conventional, the responsible line. To some, such immovable restraint is eternally admirable. To others, the display is too staid, too joyless, too sober.

Venus in Capricorn = Basic love nature. Responses to love and affection are dignified, decorous and revealed only behind locked doors. No one is admitted to the inner sanctum of intimacy until reciprocation has been proffered and proven — preferably in triplicate. Nothing is said or done from whim or caprice which dispenses with doubt and bolsters security. But later some recipients may decide Capricorn love is as sombre as the Rock of Ages itself.

Mars in Capricorn = Basic sex nature. Physical energies and passions are kept under rock-like restraint until shaken free by the proper person at the proper time in the proper place. Then the switch from sobriety to sensuality is as earth-shattering as it is unexpected. The sex drive is thus heavily repressed, but forever watching and waiting for the moment when it can throw off its load of inhibitions and find release. The other austere lovers of the zodiac can cope. More urgent spirits look elsewhere.

Love Lines for Love Signs

No. 10. Capricorn . . . the Goat personality Type Male

Here's how HE feels about love. HE's into prudent picking.

'Bright boys almost always know
'That RED means STOP and GREEN means GO!
'The shade that meets with most distortion
'IS that AMBER wink of CAUTION!'

No. 11.   The Air Sign of Aquarius
Symbol: the Striding figure of the Water-Bearer.
Behavioural keyword: 'I know!'
Classification: Positive fixed.

Sun in Aquarius = *Basic life attitude.* Fundamental approach to living is fraternal, progressive, independent, extroverted, and dogmatically different. Off-beat philosophies, eccentric characters and the brave, new world over the rainbow, turn this type on. If unrestrained by other planets in the natal map, the attendant condescension, perversity and studied detachment turn others off.

Moon in Aquarius = *Basic emotional attitude.* Emotional reactions are dispassionate, erratic and airily friendly. Feelings automatically subject themselves to the rule of the intellect and so are never ungovernable or based on narrow-minded understanding. To some, such perpetual cool is delightfully refreshing. To others, the display is too static, too remote, too superhuman.

Venus in Aquarius = *Basic love nature.* Responses to love and affection are attractively light, intriguingly aloof and undemanding. The stance taken is more that of a brother or sister than an intimate and even the closest relationship has the same fraternal flavour. But later some recipients may decide they wish to be more than Aquarius's perennial 'best friend'.

Mars in Aquarius = *Basic sex nature.* Physical energies and passions are likewise cooled off by the intervention of reason but this time with less success. Vital forces do not take kindly to being channelled through the mind and so reveal themselves in cranky, contentious and fanatically unconventional ways. The sex drive is thus enterprising, angry with itself and often close to dying of starvation. The other super-cool lovers of the zodiac can cope. Hotter spirits depart.

Love Lines for Love Signs

No. 11. Aquarius . . . the Water Bearer personality Type Female

Here's how SHE feels about love. SHE's into intellectualized emotions.

> 'Conversation is an art
> 'Which every male should master.
> 'Being macho-esque but mute
> 'Is what *I* term disaster.
>
> 'So try to learn to verbalize
> 'Your hang-ups, kinks, the lot!
> 'Then, IF there's time by 4 a.m.
> 'We'll THINK about the cot!'

No. 12   The Water Sign of Pisces
Symbol: the Linked-Together figure of the two Fish.
Behavourial keyword: 'I believe!'
Classification: Negative mutable.

Sun in Pisces = Basic life attitude. Fundamental approach to living is kindly, sympathetic, introverted, amazingly sensitive and impractical. Romantic dreams, intuitive understanding and situations where neither weighty will-power nor rational thought are needed turn this type on. If unrestrained by other planets in the natal map, the attendant changefulness, gullibility and improvidence turn others off.

Moon in Pisces = Basic emotional attitude. Emotional reactions are tender, gently felt and naturally submissive. Feelings dominate every thought, every action, forever washing like waves over consciousness. To some such boundless depths of sensitivity indicate equally boundless rapport. To others, the display is too undirected, too formless, too wish-washy.

Venus in Pisces = Basic love nature. Responses to love and affection are many-splendoured, lyrical and highly temperamental. Reality never intrudes on the romantic idyll and the cold, cruel world beyond is always viewed through sea-green spectacles. But later some recipients may decide the occasional glance at hard facts is the necessary evil which keeps bailiffs away.

Mars in Pisces = Basic sex nature. Physical energies and passions repeat the same unreality, immersing themselves in a sea of hopes and gentle fantasies where the storms of life never rage. The sex drive is thus diffused and confused, yearning for sensual and spiritual fusion with the soulmate yet forever drifting apart again. The other dream-possessed lovers of the zodiac can cope. Less sentimental spirits dash for the shore.

Love Lines for Love Signs

No. 12. Pisces . . . the Fish Personality Type Male

Here's how HE feels about love. HE's into dreamworld drifting.

'Your champagne glass on my bedside table?
'Two cigarettes stubbed in a tray?
'These are the clues from which I am able
'To deduce how we spent yesterday.

Now, we've looked at the inter-action of the personal planets in their signs, observing the often contrary traits they mix together in the personalities of those we care about and ourselves, we'll turn our microscope to the home scene. That will take us a long step further, because the marriage of our parents, the family scene we grew up within, both throw clearer light on our adult dreams of domestic bliss. But even at this still very early stage in our research into synastry, you will have begun to see just how staggeringly complex human nature and hence human relationships really are.

How *do* you cope with the glaring contradictions in behaviour of an individual born, say, with Sun in Aries, Moon in Cancer, Venus in Aries and Mars in Gemini? All that rushing in where angels fear to tread in life style and love style (Sun/Venus in Aries). Then the sudden collapse into tearful and clinging emotional display (Moon in Cancer). Then a mind-blowing switch-back to light, bright, dispassionate sex (Mars in Gemini).

Not easy, I know. And many charts do show contradictions in behaviour every bit as confusing as those or more so. But learning how to handle contrary reactions in ourselves and our intimates is precisely what we're here for!

Quick reference check-points
Plus or Minus Indicators to Compatibility

1. Planets posited in the sign of the Ram:

Co-operate well with any other planets in Aries, Leo or Sagittarius. The positive, self-assertive, energetic approach is shared by all.

Clash most obviously with any other planets in Cancer, Libra or Capricorn. Each thinks the other too egotistical.

Combine reasonably well with any other planets in Gemini and Aquarius. Their light, bright intellectualism attracts fiery Aries.

Create a wary stand-off with any other planets in Taurus, Virgo, Pisces or Scorpio. To Aries, the intensity of their involvement is smothering.

2. Planets posited in the sign of the Bull:

Co-operate well with any other planets in Taurus, Virgo, Capricorn. The indirect, self-controlled, cautious approach is shared by all.

Clash most obviously with any other planets in Leo, Scorpio or Aquarius. Each thinks the other stubbornly self-opinionated.

Combine reasonably well with any other planets in Cancer or Pisces. Their deep, comforting sensitivity attracts earthy Taurus.

Create a wary stand-off with any other planets in Aries, Sagittarius, Gemini or Libra. To Taurus, their impulsive adventurousness is disconcerting.

3. Planets posited in the sign of the Twins:

Co-operate well with any other planets in Gemini, Libra or Aquarius. The 'let's-keep-it-light-and-bright' approach is shared by all.

Clash most obviously with any other planets in Virgo, Sagittarius or Pisces. Each thinks the other too irritatingly hypocritical.

Combine reasonably well with any other planets in Aries or Leo. Their enthusiastic arrogance amuses airy Gemini.

Create a wary stand-off with any other planets in Taurus, Cancer, Scorpio or Capricorn. To Gemini, their heavy-handed predictability is dreary.

4. Planets posited in the sign of the Crab:

Co-operate well with any other planets in Cancer, Scorpio or Pisces. The 'still-waters-run-deep' approach is shared by all.

Clash most obviously with any other planets in Aries, Libra or Capricorn. Each thinks the other maddeningly egotistical.

Combine reasonably well with any other planets in Taurus or Virgo. Their passive strength comforts watery Cancer.

Create a wary stand-off with any other planets in Gemini, Leo, Sagittarius or Aquarius. To Cancer, their careless spontaneity is alarming.

5. Planets posited in the sign of the Lion:

Co-operate well with any other planets in Aries, Leo or Sagittarius. The 'up-and-at-'em' approach is shared by all.

Clash most obviously with any other planets in Taurus, Scorpio or

Aquarius. Each thinks the other as stubborn as a cartload of mules.

Combine reasonably well with any other planets in Gemini or Libra. Their sophisticated sparkle intrigues fiery Leo.

Create a wary stand-off with any other planets in Cancer, Virgo, Capricorn or Pisces. To Leo, their lack of interest in fireworks is disappointing.

6. Planets posited in the sign of the Virgin:

Co-operate well with any other planets in Taurus, Virgo or Capricorn. The 'down-to-earth-and-tin-tacks' approach is shared by all.

Clash most obviously with any other planets in Gemini, Sagittarius or Pisces. Each thinks the other has the wrong set of values.

Combine reasonably well with any other planets in Cancer or Scorpio. Their torrents of emotion make Virgo feel needed.

Create a wary stand-off with any other planets in Aries, Leo, Libra or Aquarius. To Virgo, their disdain for plain facts is horrifying.

7. Planets posited in the sign of the Scales:

Co-operate most easily with any other planets in Gemini, Libra or Aquarius. The 'let's-do-it-the-Company-way' approach is shared by all.

Clash most obviously with any other planets in Aries, Cancer or Capricorn. Each thinks the other is one-pointed in the wrong direction.

Combine reasonably well with any other planets in Leo or Sagittarius. Their friendly warmth appeals to companionable Libra.

Create a wary stand-off with any other planets in Taurus, Virgo, Scorpio or Pisces. To Libra, their thinking is much too subjective.

8. Planets posited in the sign of the Scorpion:

Co-operate most easily with any other planets in Cancer, Scorpio or Pisces. The 'Feelings-first, Thinking-second' approach is shared by all.

Clash most obviously with any other planets in Taurus, Leo or Aquarius. Each thinks the other is stuck in the stupidest rut.

Combine reasonably well with any other planets in Capricorn or Virgo. Their total reliability attracts doubting Scorpio.

Create a wary stand-off with any other planets in Aries, Gemini, Libra or Sagittarius. To Scorpio, their lack of interest in emotional issues is deflating.

9. Planets posited in the sign of the Centaur:

Co-operate most easily with any other planets in Aries, Leo or Sagittarius. The 'let's-get-cracking' approach is shared by all.

Clash most obviously with any other planets in Gemini, Virgo or Pisces. Each adds up to double trouble for the other.

Combine reasonably well with any other planets in Libra or Aquarius. Their easy sociability appeals to party-loving Sagittarius.

Create a wary stand-off with any other planets in Taurus, Cancer, Scorpio or Capricorn. To Sagittarius, their single-mindedness is confining.

10. Planets posited in the sign of the Goat:

Co-operate most easily with any other planets in Taurus, Virgo or Capricorn. 'The work-till-the-sun-sets' approach is shared by all.

Clash most obviously with any other planets in Aries, Cancer or Libra. Each thinks the other is concerned with nothing but its own ends.

Combine reasonably well with any other planets in Scorpio or Pisces. Their depth of feeling refreshes disciplined Capricorn.

Create a wary stand-off with any other planets in Gemini, Leo, Sagittarius or Aquarius. To Capricorn, their application to the task in hand lacks dedication.

11. Planets posited in the sign of the Water-Bearer:

Co-operate most easily with any other planets in Gemini, Libra or Aquarius. the 'let's-think-it-through' approach is shared by all.

Clash most obviously with any other planets in Taurus, Scorpio or Leo. Each considers the other incapable of understanding there are two sides to everything.

Combine reasonably well with any other planets in Aries or Sagittarius. Their try-anything philosophy intrigues unconventional Aquarius.

Create a wary stand-off with any other planets in Cancer, Virgo, Capricorn or Pisces. To Aquarius, their concern with the personal rather than the impersonal is narrow.

12. Planets posited in the sign of the Fish:

Co-operate most easily with any other planets in Cancer, Scorpio or Pisces. The 'let's-play-this-hunch' approach is shared by all.

Clash most obviously with any other planets in Gemini, Virgo or Sagittarius. Each thinks the other sees too many different points of view.

Combine reasonably well with any other planets in Taurus, or Capricorn. Their solid insistence on the realities guides unworldly Pisces.

Create a wary stand-off with any other planets in Aries, Leo, Libra or Aquarius. To Pisces, their pursuit of material pleasures is unevolved.

CHAPTER TWO

The Home Base:
Childhood Conditioning Versus
Adult Expectation in Relationships

'I thought this was a book about love and sexual relationships. Why bother with what went on when we were still peering over the sides of our prams?' This is the sort of question readers not familiar with precise psychological assessment of individual personality may well be asking. So, let's sum it up in one sentence:

Your earliest memories of what life and love amount to form the building blocks (smooth or jagged) which set the foundation upon which your adult hopes and expectations of affection, sexual satisfaction and partnership are based.

Why? Because when you were a child, you could not help being imprinted with the environment you found yourself in. The particular personalities of your parents . . . the type of home they created . . . whether they loved or wanted you . . . your position in the family group with or without brothers/sisters . . . the kind of marriage you observed in action. Irrespective of your chronological age now, each of these impressions, for good or ill, remains in the subconscious, driving you to behave accordingly.

Hence, although your adult thinking mind may be telling you loudly and often that the *only* thing you want in life is a happy, rewarding relationship . . . your childhood conditioning may be surreptitiously burrowing away down in the subconscious, steadily undermining your entire personality impact, pushing you towards mismatches and disappointment. 'Remember Dad and Mum screaming at each other over the breakfast table?' The subsconscious whispers sneakily into your inner ear. 'That's marriage for you! Team up with someone and watch it happen to *you*'. Or 'OK, look around and name *anyone* you know who's got a worthwhile relationship'! Or 'You always were an also-ran in the family stakes. Whatever gave you the idea someone could possibly care about *you?'*

Variations on these hopelessly negative themes are the hidden-away causes of misery and unhappiness in and out of relationships, because they generate rejecting vibes, 'Don't touch me' signals that you may be quite unaware of in your conscious mind but which potential partners pick up. So until you come to grips with them — and we all have these themes whispering away inside us in one form or another — they will drive you into relationships that are the outward and awful reflection of their inherent negativity.

As ever, your horoscope chart will spotlight such trouble-spots and place the tools in your hands to dig them out if you try. But before discussing the type of planetary positions and aspects to consider, I propose to spend a little longer on the psychological implications of early upbringing. This, I concede, is not usual in an astrological textbook. But, as mentioned earlier, the usual astrological textbook is definitely not what I set out to write. Neither do I adhere to the views of some schools of astrological thought who maintain that every conceivable calculation and every imaginable aspect of planetary link must be chewed over before a word of interpretation is uttered. This approach merely — and especially from my standpoint as a psychologist — confuses the emerging personality picture.

If you know just what you're looking for in the horoscope chart and understand the way to correlate the often conflicting personality pointers it reveals, the simplified methods I suggest in this book *will* give you the right answers. As with so many talents from figure skating to higher mathematics, the acquisition of skill makes the hardest task look easy!

Astrology and Psychology: Where's the Connection?

Many people ask this question, especially if their only acquaintance with astrology has been the meaningless 'star' columns in the popular press. You may be wondering, too, what is the fundamental difference between psychologist/astrologers and ordinary astrologers. The answer is simple — years of training in scientific personality analysis at the academic level.

Of course, astrology and psychology are natural allies because both sciences set out to penetrate the secrets of human behaviour — which is why so many leading practitioners nowadays are university-trained psychologists like myself. As Jeff Mayo, Principal of the London Faculty of Astrological Studies put it in his classic textbook, *Teach Yourself Astrology*: 'Astrology as practised today by trained consultants, by its correlation to modern psychology, eradicates muddle-headed theorising and fortune-telling sensationalism.'

Thus you *won't* find (as you construct your Compatibility Analyses by the methods set out in this book) any of the wild predictions or negative statements which fortune-teller type astrologers deal in. You *will* find the necessary self-knowledge that can help you turn your relationships into what you *want* them to be, because that is how all qualified psychologist/astrologers interpret the horoscope chart.

As you work through your analyses, each personality pointer is set out in much the same manner as the results of psychological testing. Each of these pointers shows you which parts of your innate character and your partner's amount to assets, and which parts indicate faults you'll both need to work on overcoming.

It's also worth mentioning that all psychologist/astrologers, including myself, abide by the Hippocratic Oath which reads (in brief):

> I will not give 'readings', 'tell fortunes' or make predictions to satisfy the cravings of the curious, nor will I seek to astound or mystify; but will give advice only to those who have a problem regarding which they know they need help and seek it; and instead of prophesying an answer, I will endeavour to instil the right thinking that will contribute to avoiding or minimising an unfavourable condition which I see in operation, interpreting such in terms as influences rather than events, and at all times teaching a philosophy of Free Will and emotional self-control that is the absolute opposite of Fatalism and Predestination.

(This oath is set out in full in the *Encyclopaedia of Astrology* by Nicholas de Vore.)

So you will see as you read that this book is specifically planned to show you how to apply psychological insight into human motivation as you work with astrological data so that the final blueprint of personality you reveal is well-drawn, clear and accurate. No muddles! No fortune-teller-type sensationalism!'

I stress the points set out in the Hippocratic Oath heavily because as the popularity of astrology escalates at a phenomenal rate, so do the numbers of 'practitioners' who bring shame and ridicule to the science through their own ineptitude, shoddy work or pursuit of what the Americans call 'the fast buck'. Often, I have been shown appalling examples of their efforts. These are two recent ones from scores I could quote.

One so-called 'professional' astrologer (who had also set up as a teacher) informed a student that 'daylight-saving time did not matter in chart calculation'. Another client was told by yet another of these ill-trained phonies that her husband would soon go to gaol — simply because he happened to have the planet Mars in his 12th house!

Both these statements are positively idiotic but they serve as a warning to all astrology students and possible future practitioners.

In my view, students and practitioners of astrology who have little or no understanding of human psychology usually come up with analyses that are superficial or without integration at best — dangerously misleading or ridiculously contradictory at worst.

So don't just flip through the introductory section to this chapter. As you read, think back—back and back and back in time to your own earliest memories which usually start at about the age of 3. Note them down as they flash through your mind. Then have them ready to compare to the planetary indicators which turn the searchlights onto your own childhood scene.

At times, you may find these searchlights uncomfortably bright as they focus on selected scenes from the long (and sometimes sad) journey from childhood dreams to adult realities. But don't switch them off! The more you allow yourself to remember about your origins, the better you'll be able to understand precisely who and what turned you into the individual you are today.

It's equally valuable to note that memories and environmental impressions begin conditioning human behaviour from the very moment of birth. Actually, some researchers take the moment as far back as conception to examine pre-natal influences on the developing personality *before* it emerges from the womb; e.g. Was the expectant mother fearful? Did she genuinely want a child?

In any event, the only real difference between what children think and see as compared to adults is the ability to articulate such feelings and process them — whether they add up to love, joy, anger, fear or grief — into what is regarded as an acceptably civilized response. To illustrate: I remember one of my psychology lecturers in my university student days saying to his class: 'Let's go and walk by a children's playground and see how we would act if we were honest.' Or, in other words, to see human beings behaving as they feel, i.e. naturally and spontaneously.

Of course, as we grow into adults, we gradually realize society tends to frown on such spontaneous bursts of feeling. That it simply isn't done, for example, to rush up and hug people just because we like their looks. Although, I well remember a young professional man with a chart that displayed a pretty ferocious mix of Aries impulsiveness and Scorpio sexuality who did just that. When these two unbridled signs got control, he really would rush up and embrace strange females in public places — often with catastrophic results!

Yet, on the other hand, to keep too tight a rein on our natural responses to others can be just as catastrophic in the long term, making us appear stiff, inhibited, unlovable. But, so much for the background of what we're about to tackle. Now, let's look over the horoscope charts of ourselves, our nearest and dearest and begin our trip back to childhood via the 4th house.

Special note for new students

To make the very best use of this whole chapter (and the rest of this book), you must have horoscope charts of yourself and those you care about — so you can check compatibility pointers as you read. If you don't have these charts available, you should now take one of the following steps:

● *Either* learn the techniques of chart construction from my companion book *How to Astro-Analyse Yourself and Others* (also published by the Aquarian Press) and erect the charts you require yourself.

● *Or* buy a computer chart. These are obtainable in most major towns and cities from computer services which specialize in astrological printouts. Computer charts are usually quite inexpensive and show the planetary positions, house cusps, etc. However, planets are sometimes designated by abbreviations of their names instead of by their symbols; e.g. in a computer chart, Venus may be shown as VEN instead of ♀.

Child's Eye View

There's an old proverb — Spanish, I think — which says: 'In the end is the beginning'. This sums up neatly what psychoanlaysts and psychologists (including me) regard as the end result of childhood conditioning on adult behaviour.

Using standard diagnostic techniques and personality testing, one can probe for hours in search of the childhood story because, if unhappy, these memories are likely to be heavily repressed and the subject will not, or cannot, put them into words. Yet the horoscope chart, when correctly calculated and interpreted, reveals the early history in a flash — as vividly as if a powerful beam had been trained upon it.

We are all, of course, the product of our original environment which may or may not suit our inherited characteristics. Unless we were reared by adults other than our natural parents, both hereditary traits and childhood environment are determined by the male and female who produced us.

The early environmental picture is always indicated by the 4th house: the sign on its cusp, the planets posited therein, and their aspects. Hence, if you're interested in finding out what childhood influences created the adult 'You' in cold, hard fact, start your excavations into the past with a study of your 4th house. Bear in mind, moreover, what you learn may not always tally with what your conscious mind prefers to remember. For example, if your childhood really did add up to hell on wheels, your conscious mind isn't going to be too keen to admit this revelation, especially if it conflicts with the adult self-image you seek to project.

So, why drag it all out, kicking and struggling, into the light of day, you may ask? Because until you do just that, the past is pretty adept at screwing up the future!

Here are a few pointers to start you off in unravelling the secrets of the 4th, sometimes tagged the 'nadir' in astrological texts, before we list precise definitions.

● *The sign on its cusp* will often represent the sign or element of the dominant parent. It will show which parent 'wore the pants' in conditioning your behaviour and that's not necessarily the one who appeared to deliver all the orders. The cusp sign will also give a hint as to the type of adult home your early conditioning urges you to establish.

● *Any planet occupying the 4th* will supply further indications. Pluto there implies power struggles in the domestic scene. Neptune points to peculiar conditions, perhaps a skeleton in the family cupboard! Uranus turns the home upside down and inside out with his usual breakneck speed, changing the atmosphere, the occupants, the place of residence endlessly. Saturn suggests hardship, financial or emotional, an authoritarian set-up. These few examples illustrate what you should look for and remind you that any of the other six planets, when posited in the 4th, will contribute their own distinctive influence.

- Remember, too, that the 4th is one of the *angular houses* in the chart, thus bearing heavily on each life pattern. If planets in the 4th for example, make hard aspects to the 10th, a bitter tug-o-war between the demands of the home and the demands of the career/occupation usually results.

- Frequently, also, you'll discover *the planet ruling the sign of one of your parents* esconced in the 4th, thereby sharpening the influence of that parent. To illustrate: my mother was an Aquarian, my father a Libran with a Pisces Ascendant. In my chart, Pisces sits on the 4th house cusp and Uranus, ruler of Aquarius, is posited there. I was well into early adulthood before I was able to stop acting like the Aquarian type Mother expected me to be!

Much, much more can be gleaned from correlating the 4th house picture with the rest of the chart but before we leave these introductory comments, here are a couple of quotes to set you cogitating about your own beginnings. The first is from an English writer, the Libran Oscar Wilde:

> When we are children, we love our parents. When we become adults, we judge them and rarely, if ever, forgive them.

(A daunting thought, since all of us have once been children, and many of us become parents too.) The second is from an American novelist whose name I can't recall:

> It's *never* too late to have a happy childhood!

I like that one because it demonstrates that even if your own childhood added up to a genuine, old-fashioned can of worms that you daren't touch — it's never too late to reach for the tin-opener.

Once you've taken a long, hard look at your beginnings via your 4th house, you'll see it *and* you in a new light and understand that your parents were only reacting to their 4th house pressures too!

Now to look at each of the 4th house cusps in your own charts and the needs they postulate in turn. But before you read the following cusp data, check the signs of your parents and the elements each represents. Then do the same for your partner. If reared by adoptive parents or a step-parent, note down their signs and elements and also those of the natural parents if known.

Remember, the cusp of the 4th house will give the first clues as to the type of environment into which each individual is born. And, at the same time, it offers a preview of what the home scene will be throughout adult life as well.

The Sign on the 4th — What Sort of Home Base Does it Signify?

N.B. We use the word 'You' throughout the following for easier reading. When considering other people's charts, change it in your mind to 'He' or 'She.

1. *When you spot a FIRE SIGN on the 4th house cusp* — i.e. Aries, Leo or Sagittarius — it implies often a fire-type parent and *literally* a fiery atmosphere in the early domestic scene. Spontaneity, vitality, warmth for the plus points. Flare-ups, aggressive confrontations, lack of supportiveness for the minus points.
2. *When you spot an AIR SIGN on the 4th house cusp* — i.e. Gemini, Libra or Aquarius — it implies often an air-type parent and *literally* an airy atmosphere in the early domestic scene. Intellectuality, easy communication, mental stimulation for the plus points. Inconsistency, over-objectivity, detachment for the minus points.
3. *When you spot an EARTH SIGN on the 4th house cusp* — i.e. Taurus, Virgo or Capricorn — it implies often an earth-type parent and *literally* an earthy atmosphere in the early domestic scene. Practicality, responsibility, solidarity for the plus points. Narrowness, addiction to routine, over-caution for the minus points.
4. *When you spot a WATER SIGN on the 4th house cusp* — i.e. Cancer, Scorpio or Pisces — it implies often a water-type parent and *literally*

a watery atmosphere in the early domestic scene. Sensitivity, emotional rapport, protectiveness for the plus points. Instability, over-emotionalism, secretiveness for the minus points.

Now, examine your own chart and think about the 4th house cusp in relation to your own unbringing. If the element indicating the home atmosphere was incompatible with your personality as shown by your chart, it infers a somewhat uncomfortable early environment, with childhood memories possibly repressed yet still leaving a residual tendency to seek out exactly the same atmosphere with love partners and those with whom you share your adult home. On the other hand, if the element was compatible, the childhood scene was likely to be more reassuring, the memories happier and more easily recalled and thus the chances of creating the right type of adult home significantly improved. You'll understand this better if you've thoroughly grasped the elemental symbolism set out in Chapter 1.

To illustrate further: A *fiery* home set-up often feels too 'hot' for predominantly earth- or water-type children, yet can prove energizing to predominantly air- and fire-type offspring.

An *airy* home set-up often feels too 'cold' for predominantly earth- or water-type children yet can prove stimulating for predominantly air- and fire-type offspring.

An *earthy* home set-up often feels too 'heavy' for predominantly air- or fire-type children yet can prove strengthening for predominantly earth- and water-type offspring.

A *watery* home set-up often feels too 'wet' for predominantly air- or fire-type children yet can prove nurturing to predominantly water- and earth-type offspring.

Now compare your own 4th house cusp indicator with that of your love partner. You'll see at a glance what you've both experienced in your early days and the kind of home you're still instinctively seeking. If the two differ markedly, here comes the first of your cohabitation problems.

Let's say you're accustomed to an earthy home — parental duties and responsibilities always top of the priority list, not much entertaining, good, plain food and no frills. Then let's say your partner was raised in an airy home — everybody talking, exchanging ideas, people coming and going, parties that rage all night. Clearly, both of you are going to have to compromise on your visions of Home Sweet Home or the foundations will start rocking before you've finished putting up the curtains.

Compatibility, like charity, begins at home and something as comparatively trivial as habitual untidiness can wreck your hopes of conjugal bliss every bit as quickly as something as drastic as habitual infidelity.

Gods in Orbit — Planetary Symbolism

Newcomers to astrological studies often find the role of the personal planets in determining natal traits and behavioural patterns hard to grasp. You'll find it much easier to follow if you remember always that astrology is a language of symbols and why the personal planets, other than the Sun and Moon, bear the names they do. Each was named after one of the gods of the ancient world. They were chosen because the specified god symbolized the traits that each planet confers. So let's follow the idea through and look at them one by one.

Mercury: In his winged helmet and winged sandals, Mercury was the fleet-footed messenger of the gods, soaring here and there through the stratosphere, never still for a minute, communicating, spreading ideas, exchanging information and gossip. *And* sometimes indulging in a spot of stirring and hassling.

His activities hence were invariably mental, using both the written and the spoken word. Thus, astrologically, he governs individual mentality, indicating by his sign, house position and aspects in your horoscope chart just how your mind works — whether your thinking is serious or lightweight, whether you respond quickly or slowly to intellectual stimuli.

Venus: With her clinging robes, flowing tresses and often enigmatic expression, Venus was the breathtakingly beautiful goddess of love, courted and admired by her fellow deities, capricious in bestowing her favours, showering the delights of love on some, refusing them to others, surrounded always with beauty, music, ease and plenty.

Her activities hence concentrated on the softer, gentler side of close liaisons. Thus, astrologically, she governs individual needs in love, friendship and affection, indicating by her sign, house position and aspects just how you respond to those cared about — whether your loving is warm or cold, whether you hide your feelings or let them show.

Mars: With his red battle dress, tufted helmet and ever-brandished sword, Mars was the fiery, fierce and violent god of war and sex, racing hither and thither in his chariot, smiting down all who opposed him and so often irresistible to mortal women and goddesses alike. His activities were hence predominantly physical, applying his energies to sexual conquest and personal combat alike. Thus, astrologically, he governs individual sexuality and physical force, indicating by his sign, house position and aspects in your horoscope chart just how high is your level of energy and sexuality — whether you react passionately or coolly, whether you're a predominantly physical person or not.

The same mythological symbolism applies to the other five planets. If you're interested in looking them up in encyclopaedias you'll find each derives its name and characteristics from Ancient Greek and Roman deities.

Visualize this god-type image when you're working with the planets in any chart and you'll discover it's a lot simpler to remember which does what. Say, for example, you find Mercury in favourable aspect to Venus. Imagine the fast-moving, quick-thinking celestial messenger holding hands — as it were — with the queen of love and beauty. The picture speaks for itself! An individual with that aspect isn't going to run into much trouble in ensuring others agree with his/her ideas — because they'll be expressed so swiftly and beautifully.

Fourth House Planets: The Stories they Tell

Before we list the specific influence of planets in the 4th house from the standpoint of domestic expectations and their ultimate bearing on compatibility, toss out of your mind now any old-fashioned tags you may have collected from older-style texts. Regrettably, books are still around (mostly written before the precise psychological impact of each planet was understood) which tag planet aspects with ominous adjectives such as 'adverse' or 'very adverse' and spine-chilling terms like 'malefic' or 'malignant'. Thus the unfortunate souls, lumbered with a sack full of these, gain the impression they might as well give up now and beat the rush of disasters.

Further, that type of writing usually comes down just as ponderously on the bright side, prophesying a lifetime of champagne and roses if a chart shows a majority of good aspects. Thus the happy recipients of such heavenly favour are invariably knocked into a quivering heap when the promised manna from above fails to fall on schedule.

In my view, no planet and no aspect is any better or worse than the next one. Whether it will stir up strife or bring easier living depends on how its energy is handled by its 'owner'.

Fourth House Data at a Glance

The focus on the 4th	Reveals all homes from infancy to end of life; type of domestic conditions attracted or desired; individuals with whom homes are shared.
The planets in the 4th	Add further emphasis on above; bolster or baulk domestic objectives; introduce contrary or cohesive attitudes.
The aspects to the 4th	Link up other houses (i.e. life sectors) with the home; easy aspects offer support from other out-of-the-home activities; awkward aspects create powerful drives that compete with domestic needs.

Sun in 4th. Implies *self-image* largely derived from home experiences, absorbed in childhood, projected into adult behaviour. Strong early influence likely from father or father figures. Sense of personal security dependent on supportive home conditions. Rarely a natural roamer.

Moon in 4th. Implies *emotional well-being* largely derived from home experiences, absorbed in childhood, projected into adult behaviour. Strong early influence from mother or mother figures likely. Moods and behaviour immediately reflect domestic unrest. Often hard to please.

Mercury in 4th. Implies *way of thinking* largely derived from home experiences, absorbed in childhood, projected into adult behaviour. Intellectual stimulation sought from intimates and/or family. Easily becomes rattled if partner uncommunicative. Restless attitudes may engender domestic bickering.

Venus in 4th. Implies *expression of love/affection* largely derived from home experiences, absorbed in childhood, projected into adult behaviour.

Peace and pleasantness sought in domestic atmosphere. Easily disturbed by disharmony or aggression. Prefers diplomacy to confrontation.

Mars in 4th. Implies *sexual behaviour and physical reactions* largely derived from home experiences, absorbed in childhood, projected into adult behaviour. Force and energy applied to domestic scene. Would rather fight than arbitrate. May create stormy scenes.

Jupiter in 4th. Implies *natural optimism and use of opportunities* largely derived from home experiences, absorbed in childhood, projected into adult behaviour. Not willing to accept narrow lifestyle or thrift from intimates. Likes to impress through standard of home. May exhibit a buy-now-pay-later attitude.

Saturn in 4th. Implies *sense of personal discipline and self-control* largely derived from home experiences, absorbed in childhood, projected into adult behaviour. Desire to stabilize and restrict home activities. Possible early deprivation, emotional or financial, from parental behaviour. May exhibit over-austere, dogmatic attitudes. Often finds it hard to give.

Uranus in 4th. Implies *development of personal independence and demand for freedom* largely derived from home experiences, absorbed in childhood, projected into adult behaviour. Often rebellious, rarely domestic type. Many changes of home likely throughout life. Usually don't-fence-me-in attitudes.

Neptune in 4th. Implies *spiritual needs and illusions* largely derived from home experiences, absorbed in childhood, projected into adult behaviour. Inspiration and spiritual rapport sought from intimates. May suggest well-hidden, skeleton in family cupboard. Possibility of fantasy element entering into domestic concerns. Often daydreamer attitudes.

Pluto in 4th. Implies *compulsions and obsessions* largely derived from home experiences, absorbed in childhood, projected into adult behaviour. Genuine co-operation with family or partners often difficult. Drastic upheavals in domestic affairs possible. Entire life likely to be transformed by power struggles within the home. Often do-it-my-way attitudes.

Aspects to the 4th: Clues to the Past

As we have now noted, the Sun, Moon and the eight other planets each play a vital role in establishing compatibility with respect to domestic expectations and the past experiences which channel such expectations. But there's still one more essential point to consider: the aspects planets in the 4th make to planets in other houses of the horoscope chart.

For readers not fully familiar with astrological data, a complete list of planetary aspects appears in Chapter 4 of my companion book *How to Astro-analyse Yourself and Others.* To check your partner's planetary aspects and your own, please refer to this list or look up any authoritative astrological text. I suggest this because the list of possible planetary aspects is too extensive to repeat in detail in this section. So we'll just look at a few pointers to ensure that you are on the right track.

Remember: The most significant helpful aspects are: some conjunctions, trines, sextiles. The most significant challenging aspects are: some conjunctions, squares and oppositions.

Now you will need to:

1.   Write down what planetary aspects appear in your own chart.
2.   Then do the same for your partner and/or family.
3.   Then compare both sets of aspects.

At this stage of your compatibility analyses, we are considering specifically planetary impact on home affairs.

Now, let's tie in all data we've assembled in this chapter and watch it in action with a married couple we'll call Harry and Helen.

Fourth house cusp. Harry has an air sign there; Helen has a water sign. Not too good. Definitions of what adds up to a satisfying home life differ markedly. He wants intellectual stimulation, because he was conditioned to expect it. She wants emotional understanding, for the same reason.

Planets in the 4th. Harry has the Moon there. Helen has Uranus. Here we have something of a turnabout. His domestic-duties mother dominated his early life; thus he sees all women through her image. Helen is neither dominating nor domestic like his mother so he feels emotionally dissatisfied. He tries to pressurize Helen into responding to his needs. She resists because Uranus will not take restraint. Hence neither feels comfortable in the home together.

Aspects to the 4th. Harry's Moon squares Mercury in his 12th house. Helen's Uranus opposes Mars in her 10th house. The plot thickens, problems multiply. He cannot easily verbalize his emotional needs; what he says, especially to women close to him, is not necessarily what he means. Her lack of domesticity is heightened by Mars' force in concentrating physical energies on career. She feels hemmed in, misunderstood.

The above is only a brief indicator of this couple's compatibility because for now we have kept our searchlight trained solely on the home scene as shown by the 4th house picture. The numerous other factors which have to be taken into account in assessing relationships plus complete Compatibility Rating Tables will be set out in our complete example in Chapter 6. But, as you can see, even the above indicators can reveal dangerous clash-points which have to be handled carefully by *both* partners if a relationship is to survive.

Now, take your own chart and your partner's, setting out your conclusions as we have just done for Harry and Helen. What do you see? Roses round the 4th house door or a thicket of thorns?

Of course, I am not suggesting for a moment that you strike potential partners off your love list or walk out on existing mates — just because your pick up some trouble spots in the home scene comparison. Even Harry and Helen in our example (and more about the astrological ups and downs of this pair in later chapters) did stay together for over twenty years with not all that much going for them. What I *am* suggesting is that the better you comprehend your own needs and the needs of those you care about, the better become the chances of a workable compromise being reached. And, unromantic as it sounds, the capacity to compromise is the secret of success.

No relationship between creatures as complex as human beings is ever idyllic, especially in the long-term view. Even couples who have weathered the storms of matrimony for more than fifty years will tell you this.

Now, just before we leave the 4th house story for further adventures in synastry, there are two more small twists in the plot we have to check over. The first is the dividing line between the generations — a vital factor in understanding the attitudes of your parents. Even more vital if you've a partner in mind or in the flesh who is *considerably* older or younger than you are.

Jumping over the Generation Gap

It is Pluto-massive, ponderous and inexorable — who indelibly stamps the mass consciousness of each generation by his long sojourns in each sign of the Zodiac. However, although the period that Pluto remains in any given sign averages about 20 years, the planet's orbit is erratic and hence the movement through some signs is much shorter than it is with others. So check now from your own charts, which sign Pluto occupied at the time you were born, then do the same for your parents and partners.

Below, we'll just set out the approximate time spans for each appropriate Pluto generation. You'll observe that sometimes these time spans overlap slightly. This is due to the fact that Pluto goes retrograde quite often, thus his position must be checked in the ephemeris for each person you're considering.

Pluto in Cancer generation: Most individuals born between 1912 and 1939. This group will be the parents of today's mature and youngish adults. Their gut reactions as an entire group reflect Cancer traits — i.e. security-oriented, home-and-family minded.

Pluto in Leo generation: Most individuals born betwen 1937 and 1958. This group represents most of today's younger adults. Their gut reactions as an entire group reflect Leo traits — i.e. leadership-oriented, power-minded.

Pluto in Virgo generation: Most individuals born between 1956 and 1972. This group represents most of today's adolescents and very young adults. Their gut reaction as an entire group reflect Virgo traits — i.e. work-oriented, healthy-life-minded.

Even from merely glancing through the above, you can see the potential for huge differences in subconcious programming that Pluto has induced. Concepts of family life, group memories, social standards deeply embedded in the psyche of each generation are a powerful, underlying force in moulding behaviour. Bear this in mind when you're ready to scream because your parents 'don't understand' you. Even more so, if your partner's Pluto sign is different from your own and he/she doesn't understand you either.

As novelist John Wyndham once pointed out — every one of us bears 'the invisible stigmata of our time'. And these Plutonic marks constantly evidence in many, many ways. From fashions and musical tastes to definitions of love and marriage. To illustrate: My two older daughters, although there is a twelve-year age difference between them, were both born with Pluto in Leo and thus belong to that generation. My youngest daughter, although less than three years younger than one sister, was born with Pluto in Virgo. When the chips are finally down — always Pluto's favourite moment — the two Pluto/Leos react identically, whereas the Pluto/Virgo instinctively and instantly rejects the inevitable basic histrionics of a Leo stance.

Apply this check now to those close to you. Think about it and you'll see it work every time — irrespective of what other comfortable blends or clash-points exist in your charts.

Thus the way to jump more easily over the 'Generation Gap' is to appreciate and allow for the markedly differing moulds in which each generation has been cast, especially if your partner belongs to a much later or much earlier one than you do.

To make these inbuilt moulds fit together better, whether in parental or personal relationships, takes genuine effort but it *can* be done. Then when one of those Pluto-inspired 'Moments of Truth' comes along you'll be able to ride out the maelstrom.

On Father's Lap, at Mother's Knee: What we Learn for Life

Psychologically as well as astrologically, there is no doubt that the male and female we see before us when we first arrive in this world stamp us with their images. Not surprising really when you reflect that to our infant eyes these two gigantic beings, peering down at our cots, quickly reveal themselves as the source from which 'cometh all help'. And punishment, too, for that matter.

Whether our parents be natural, adoptive or foster, they set in our developing minds indelibly forever the definition of 'what is a man' and 'what is a woman'. As a result, we judge our own masculinity or femininity against these criteria and apply the same rules to all other males and females who cross our paths in any significant manner.

Parents' individual capacity to fill whatever happens to be the accepted roles of men and women at the time we were born and in the society to which we belong makes a further imprint upon us by constructing models for our own adult behaviour. Thus if parents deviate from the standard model or engage in role reversals, the conflicting images — of what society expects and what we've actually got at either end of the dinner table — can throw us into psychological turmoil.

I often think of a psychiatrist colleague of mine who used to say with notable solemnity: *'Never* marry a man who hates his mother!' — which is just another way of putting the problem. If a man hates his mother, he will see all women as frightening, perverse, domineering authority figures, i.e. as mirror images of his mother, even when they have few or none of her traits. Indeed, I would go one better than the above quote and say: 'Never team up with anyone who hated *or* adored the parent of the opposite sex.' Both emotions are excesses and hence danger signals.

Hatred creates distortion; adoration creates worship. Both blind us to the true character of the person we hate or adore. Thus if you are a male reader, keep your radar full-on when you're dealing with a female who has either kind of father fixation. If she hated her father, you're going to look like Frankenstein every time you exhibit specifically male traits. If she adored him, you're at a disadvantage even before you start. You're competing with The Greatest Man Who Ever Lived.

The same warnings work for females dealing with males who have either kind of mother fixation. We all have enough defects of our own without carrying an overload of somebody else's.

Often, of course, hatred or adoration of a parent is seldom consciously admitted or even discussed between partners. Luckily, here as in all other parts of personality analysis, the horoscope chart will dissipate the smoke screens the conscious mind throws up to hide the naked truth — particularly through hard aspects to the Sun (Masculine Principle) or the Moon (Feminine Principle).

A female with the Sun in challenging aspects to other planets invariably finds it hard to comprehend maleness. Such aspects can point to the fact that Father wasn't there, didn't care, was too tough or too weak. To exemplify: A woman with the Sun in hard aspect to Saturn is often covertly fearful of men. She may see them as 'Hanging Judges' because that's the image of men Father passed on to her.

Again, the same goes for males with the Moon in challenging aspects to other planets. At the subconscious level, everything female may fill him with dread and uncertainty because that's the image of women Mother passed on to him. To exemplify: A man with the Moon in hard aspect to Neptune can lose himself in the labyrinth of feminine wiles at the flash of a long-lashed eye or the heave of a well-upholstered bosom.

Naturally, other factors in any chart will help to alleviate these varieties of problems, but they won't totally eradicate the effect of parental imagery. To exemplify: Even if only the Sun and Moon are in challenging aspect to each other, such a person is usually the product of a marriage where some kind of conflict existed. Hence, the male and female images themselves conflict and the result is a sense of disharmony within the self.

Certainly, a bad parental marriage is capable of creating havoc in your own concepts and expectations. But, curiously, if your parents were blissfully happy with each other, exactly the same end result can occur. They may have been too busy loving each other to bother all that much about loving their offspring. A bitter pill for some astrological types to swallow.

Or, your parent's perfect marriage may lure you into believing that's precisely what heaven has in store for you. A sad awakening if your chart dictates otherwise and you have to work like a fiend to achieve a modicum of domestic peace.

This last situation I know only too well from my own experience. My Libran father and Aquarian mother spent their time whirling airily and happily together through the intellectual stratosphere with earthy Virgoan me orbiting doggedly around them like a small but persistent satellite moon. Now, I come to think of it, though both would take a crack at me when their somewhat sporadic sense of discipline demanded, I never heard them speak an angry word to each other (hackneyed as that sounds). Not even when my father's natural Libran diplomacy was stretched to its outer limits as he skilfully navigated the eternally troubled waters surrounding my maniacally Scorpionic uncle — Mother's youngest brother. He and she waged a no-holds-barred sibling war — literally from the cradle to the grave. (Never much love lost between Aquarius and Scorpio, of course.)

Sadly, however, my father died suddenly when he was 42 and I was still in my early school years. I wouldn't go so far as to say my mother never smiled again — smiling is very much part of the Aquarian repertoire — but she mourned him unceasingly for the remaining twenty-three years of her life. On the double grave (I had the bizarre thought it rather resembled a sort of double bed), she placed the inscription 'Thy Memory Hallowed'. And to the end of her days, she rarely mentioned my father without her eyes filling with tears.

All this was pretty strong and impressive stuff for their only child.

I remember thinking: 'Isn't it wonderful for two people to care about each other like that? I can't wait to grow up and get married!' Although a still, small voice within did casually mention that the events just narrated also proved that 'loving all the way' can turn out to be a risky business.

The purpose of relating this personal story is simply that it exemplifies what I pointed out a few paragraphs earlier. Compare it to any similar situations in your own life.

My own chart was certainly not set fair for matrimonial joy since, among other factors, Pluto and Uranus were both hard at work creating planetary pressures which turned me into a totally non-domestic type, unconventional, fundamentally rebellious and unwilling to co-operate except on the surface of things. Two marriages and three children later, I finally got the message. But parental example being what it is, I never got over that childhood belief that love and marriage *ought* to be 'wonderful'.

Lastly when you start erecting charts regularly, you'll observe that yet another intriguing fact emerges. A notable sampling of individuals team up with a partner of the same Sun sign as one of his/her parents. (And, yes! The second man *I* married was a Libran — just like Dad!) In every case, such a choice is partially explicable by the fact that the particular Sun sign 'feels somehow familiar' and thus can be more easily related to. There is *always* a streak of similarity among individuals born under the same Sun sign, which will be sensed if not overtly recognized.

This choice of partners is even more likely if parental imagery was very heavily imprinted. The trouble is that the two roles (like railway tickets) are *not transferable*. What you accepted with reasonable grace from Mother or Father in the way of orders, instructions, response may be the last thing you fancy in a spouse or lover.

Quick reference check-points

Plus or Minus Indicators of Home Expectations

Ancestral links: Specific signs tend to repeat through many generations of any family, at the level of Ascendant, Sun or Moon. Go back as far as you can in your own family and note what signs reappear in succeeding generations. This exercise shows you how, astrologically as well as genetically, hereditary traits are passed on to descendants. (e.g. in the British Royal Family, the sign of Leo is one which very frequently recurs in its ancestral patterns). Or to quote from the biblical texts: 'The sins of the fathers are visited on the children. Yea, until the third and fourth generation.'

Environment v. Heredity: Psychologically speaking, it has long been established that these two powerful forces together hammer out your adult personality. In this chapter, we've seen them both at work as your chart reveals what you have inherited from parents and how their domestic scene shaped your behaviour.

Fourth house partner type: If no other planetary indicator or chart pointer suggests why you chose a particular lover/spouse, the sign on the 4th house cusp often will; e.g. your chart may exhibit little or no affinity with water-type partners, i.e. those with Cancer, Scorpio or Pisces strong in their charts, but if water is on the 4th, you will frequently find yourself drawn inexorably towards water people.

Sibling sidelights: If you had brothers/sisters sharing the home with you in childhood, a study of differing 4th house patterns will usually spotlight vastly differing responses among siblings to their early home environment; e.g. in your own eyes, childhood might be labelled as 'Golden Days' whereas your oldest sister couldn't fly the family nest fast enough. This implies the original home set-up was right and developmental for you, wrong and disintegrating for her!

Tight aspects: In examining planetary aspects, never forget the closer the orb i.e. the degrees between the two planets aspecting each other, the more intense the effect; e.g. to draw an example of planetary aspect cross-referencing from my own life again. My youngest daughter has Saturn at 0 degrees 38 minutes of Capricorn. My Moon is 0 degrees 38 minutes of Capricorn. The conjunction is exact to the minute and hence quite rare in charts. Result? My sense of maternal responsibility came on with earth-shattering force the moment she was born. Check now for similar close aspects in your own charts.

First and onlys: If you were the eldest or only child of your parents, you are likely to react more visibly to their conditioning. Partially because Mother and Father were both novices in the art of child-rearing when you arrived and hence may have transferred not only their own anxieties about it on to you — but also their personal, unrealized ambitions. This type of beginning often makes you a trier in the Achievement Race but rarely too easy to live with!

Now, we've completed our excavations into the foundations of your 4th house, we can see the process is rather like working on an archaeological dig. You never know what ancient relic of the past is going to come to light next!

I have spent a considerable amount of time on the 4th because, in my view, clear comprehension of one's beginnings are vital factors in all compatibility analyses. But, now the moment has come to open the 7th house door and observe what facts or fantasies about marriage, partnerships and all forms of permanent liaison are hiding away inside.

CHAPTER THREE

Marriage and/or Commitment . . . To Be or Not to Be?

Romantic Love

Today's there's a wedding at the Grand Hotel — really a smart affair,
From where I sit I can see the crowd, champagne and orchids everywhere.
I can see them standing hand in hand, and even the glint of her ring.
Wonderful that I don't feel sad — but then I don't feel anything.

Although those few lines are not great verse and have lost a lost in translation from their original language, I've remembered them for more than twenty years. They never fail to remind me of the awesome chain reaction of wasted opportunities and wasted lives that can follow when the wrong people marry each other. The words are part of an unfinished song written long ago by a musician I once knew and they actually tell part of his own story. He really did sit in the corner of that hotel bar and watch the girl he loved — *and* who loved him — marry someone else. Simply because he could not decide. Could not bring himself to overcome the obstacles — more imagined than real — and take the final step of commitment.

From that wedding day on, it was downhill all the way for him. Nothing spectacular. Just a slow but sure descent into dullness and despair. Deeper and deeper into self-recrimination, his subconscious mind accusing him again and again for the weakness, the hesitation that had lost him his love and his one chance of happiness. (Some people do only meet the right partner *once* in their lives.)

Yet had he looked into his chart beforehand, he would have had no doubt that his moment, his 'once-in-a-lifetime' had come. And, if he let it slip away, that mistake would have to be paid for till the end of his days. He would have seen how a dangerous mix of Aries, Pisces and Scorpio planets with Saturn and Pluto playing key roles in the drama, could manufacture situations fraught with passion, rashness and indecision. And he *could* have controlled them.

Instead, he drifted subsequently (Pisces-style) in and out of a string of unsatisfying relationships, and, years later, in and out of two pointless marriages. He fathered four children but showed little interest in them. He began drinking heavily. His creative talents dimmed. He fell victim to illnesses that are the physical manifestation of unhappiness. He spoke no less than the truth when he said: 'I don't feel *anything*.'

For some personality types, the total switch-off of *all* feelings is the favoured way of handling present anguish and continuing emotional frustration. (A heavily aspected Saturn will often imply this.) It is unquestionably effective, even though it does not always register in the conscious mind. But its permanent effects are devastatingly destructive. Life is thereafter lived — as it were — on 'automatic pilot'. Nothing matters anymore, nothing is ever cared about again. A sad story with a sad ending. Sadder still when you think that stories of what Shakespeare called 'ill-starred lovers' not only blight the lives of the pair themselves but invariably the lives of so many others too. New partners, children, people who were not to blame and had no part in it.

Am I suggesting that had this man understood his chart and found the courage to marry the girl he loved they would have lived happily ever after? Not quite, but very nearly that. So much misery and hopelessness would have been averted. So much that was wasted would have been saved. Or to quote the German philosopher Schopenhauer: 'The ultimate end of all love affairs is really more important than all the other ends of human life and is therefore quite worthy of the profound seriousness with which every one pursues it.'

Once again, throughout this chapter and indeed the entire book, we're aiming to blend trained psychological insight with astrological data in arriving at our conclusions about love and marriage. Naturally, the musician's story was not intended to assert that romantic love alone with its incredible highs is the ideal basis for successful marriage as we'll see in this and later sections. It is all too easy to love someone to distraction without liking him/her. Yet *liking* that person's lifestyle, daily habits, way of dress, etc., is important; these apparent trivia are factors that finally add up to happy or unhappy cohabitation.

For these are what you have to live with day after day after day. Constant hair in curlers (slovenliness or vanity?), dropping shirts and ties from one end of the house to the other (untidiness, lack of thought?), tooth-grinding arguments about whose duty it is to put out the rubbish bins at night. These dreary little details can finally build up into wedges large enough to crack the very foundations of relationships. Not merely for the minor irritants they are but because they point to traits that are unpleasant, unlikeable and unloveable — because they point to fundamental lack of caring for the partner.

Marriage Today — Not what It Used to Be

In beginning our exploration of individual needs/expectations in permanent union, we must understand that *no marriage is an island*. It takes place, succeeds or fails against the social background of its time — the current standards in morals, customs, religions. Today, in the late twentieth century, that background is blurry to say the least.

With the first gleams of the dawning of the Age of Aquarius back in the 1950s, the sign itself and the heavy planets engendering sweeping social change began slowly but inexorably to re-define the nature of marriage and indeed all forms of permanent commitment. Think back to those far-off days and the contrast with today's lifestyles becomes staggering, unbelievable. Instant sex, *de facto* relationships, illegitimate children were once the exception and are now rapidly approaching the rule for huge groups of individuals. So common in fact that even the Law has been forced to abandon its centuries-long stance and begin to recognize the legal rights of those who choose to live together without what used to be called 'benefit of clergy'.

So, whether we like the changes or not, we can't hide our heads in the sands of time and pretend marriage is what it used to be — i.e. lifelong commitment 'till death do us part'.

Perversely (and remembering Aquarius always likes to remake the rules) you find *de facto* partners who do stay together till death do them part while their married contemporaries snap the ties within weeks of making them.

There are, of course, numerous personality traits which explain this apparent paradox and the many others clustering round modern relationships. A major one behind the choice of *de facto* instead of legal marriage is the undeniable fact that while neither partner has any contractual rights — and marriage *is* a contract — over the other, both will usually make a greater effort to please. The fear of the slammed door, the packed suitcases, is ever-present and thus an even more powerful moderator of behaviour than it is when the marriage certificate is safely stowed in the bottom drawer.

It is always dangerous to pull one or two planetary aspects out of a chart to arrive at a final decision as to personality type or intentions. Nevertheless, I think it can be safely said that the *de facto* choice can often be sheeted home to Uranus or Neptune. Their house positions and aspects in charts will at least hint at an unquenchable demand for freedom and personal space (Uranus) or the tendency to drift into nebulous, vague involvements (Neptune).

Still, I do not think judgement on either form of permanent union is a matter for criticism or approval. I merely wish to press the point that the decision to opt for permanent cohabitation instead of marriage is *for the first time in recorded history* open to everyone who wishes to take it — with little or no public censure.

That fact alone makes late twentieth-century pairings unique and remarkable. Certainly, throughout the past there have always been some couples who lived together but they did it in the face of almost universal condemnation. The Church, the State, the Law were all united against them, thrusting them into the role of social pariahs, bohemians, or at very least apologists for their lack of marital status. Their union and offspring were denied all legal rights: society turned its back contemptuously upon them. Religions threatened them with every variety of hellfire and damnation.

Compare centuries of those kind of penalties to the attitudes of today. In little more than twenty years, widespread rejection of traditional marriage in favour of living together has revolutionized moral standards and human values. That's how fast and how radical the changes have been. Yet because what was once ignominiously termed 'living in sin' has now become so commonplace and thus familiar, we tend to forget — until we stop and think about it — just how far the social pendulum had to swing in order to make it both possible and accepted.

Perhaps, the extremity and speed of the swing becomes a little less astonishing when you realize that sudden leaping to extremes is very much the signature of Aquarius on the age we're moving into. This realization also explains in part yet another contradiction of our time. Today, in many Western societies, divorce is quicker, easier and cheaper than ever before. Remember, only as recently as last century, you required in British-governed countries an Act of Parliament to obtain divorce. Since that fact alone meant the expenditure of vast sums, followed by social ostracism and religious taboos, most people who had made their marriage beds certainly *had* to lie in them!

So why, when you can now slip out of a marriage as easily as you slipped into it, are so many younger couples so reluctant to sign on the dotted line to the sound of music? Clearly again, the onset of the Aquarian Age answers the question in part. Neither the sign of Aquarius nor its ruler Uranus fancies either traditions or binding ties and rarely hesitate to overthrow one and break the other when the need arises.

However, astrologically speaking, Aquarius/Uranus are not the only architects of present-day behaviour in relationships. It is highly significant that the swing against legal marriage began in the 1960s and escalated swiftly through the 1970s. Why? Because in those two decades the radically new mass responses and gut reactions of the Pluto/Leo Generation began to make themselves felt.

This group — born roughly between 1937 and 1958 and thus arriving at effective maturity between 1957 and 1978 — threw overboard with revolutionary gusto the conformist ideas of their Pluto/Cancer Generation parents.

As American astrologer Virginia Elenbaas pointed out in her 1974 book, *Focus on Pluto:* 'Standards of marriage, family, patriotism, education, etc. which had been blindly accepted by others were questioned by this youth, and in some cases changed so much that our social directions will never be quite the same again.'

Now, in the latter part of the 1980s, the oldest members of the Pluto/Leo generation are middle-aged and the youngest members well past their wild days too, so we can expect to see the pendulum of change swing in yet another new direction as their successors, the Pluto/Virgos, gradually wrest the sceptre of power from the Lion's grasp.

Unlike, Leo, Virgo is not a sign which looks with favour on dramatic rule-breaking or free love as a way of life. Thus when the Pluto/Virgo generation, born approximately between 1956 and 1972, become mature enough as a group to show their strengths, a return to more stable, more cool-headed relationships is at least possible.

Nevertheless, whatever our own chronological age and generation characteristics — as individuals and as members of specific social groups and cultures — every one of our marriages/unions must be coloured by this background of continuing, sometimes disorientating change.

Precisely how we handle the changes in our partnerships with others is spotlighted by the 7th house, its cusp, its planets and their aspects — not forgetting, of course, that when we arrive at the final analysis, we must also tie in the often contradictory needs and expectations which other parts of every chart indicate. All we have already looked at and all we'll work through in later chapters.

As I constantly stress to students, no single facet of personality, no one life sector must be concentrated on at the expense of the others, especially in compatibility questions. To repeat an analogy I've often used in my other books: think of the completed analysis as a tapestry of intricate design, worked with threads of vividly contrasting colours. Don't keep embroidering over and over in the same spot. If you do that, the picture becomes lumpy, distorted. It looks, and is, wrong. So don't be tempted to 'over-colour' the 7th house.

Remind yourself regularly that genuine compatibility is much more than a matter of wanting to be with someone or falling in love or getting married. The Oxford dictionary defines compatibility as 'the ability to co-exist'. Doesn't sound at all romantic, does it? But successful co-existence covers a lot of territory that has nothing to do with romance.

To begin with, note the sign on the 7th house cusp in every chart is always the opposing sign to the one on the 1st house cusp, thereby symbolizing the struggle between the self as an individual (1st) and the self as a partner (7th). Two vastly differing sets of needs and demands.

In some astrological texts, the 7th house cusp is termed the 'Descendant'. The sign on the 1st house cusp is always termed the 'Ascendant'.

There is another intriguing piece of symbolism to be gleaned from this point. The Ascendant is always calculated from the moment of birth. The moment when we enter this world as tiny, self-centred individuals, concerned solely with our own immediate needs to the point that nothing else is thought of or exists.

Yet the Ascending sign dictates the Descending sign, thereby pointing to the ways in which we must learn (often painfully) to channel the 'me-centred' attitudes we began life with into the 'us-centred' attitudes of successful partnership.

This symbolism leaps easily out of the chart when you consider that in the Hours Divisions of Horoscope, the Ascendant is assigned to the hour of sunrise — the time of dawning and days beginning. The

Descendant, accordingly, is assigned to the hour of sunset . . . the time of twilight and days ending.

In all happy, adult, enduring relationships, the selfish thrust of the unbridled ego of childhood has been jointly conquered and transcended. Or to put it in the terms of nature, the flaming reds of dawn have been softened into the rosy glow of sunset.

Signs on the Seventh: Partner Types They Attract

When you spot a *fire sign on the 7th house cusp*, it implies a pull towards fiery, ardent, spontaneous unions and sometimes towards partners with fire signs — i.e. Aries, Leo, Sagittarius — dominating their charts. Often, too, because fire fans the flames of impulse and desire, the risk of dashing into a permanent involvement *without* looking before leaping.

If one of your parents was a fire sign type *and* greatly affected your ideas about marriage, you will often find that parent's sign or element on your 7th house cusp.

● *The plus* with fire here is that it is capable of promoting warmth and spontaneity in long-term relationships.
● *The minus* with fire here is that it is equally capable of burning them out.

When you spot an *air sign on the 7th house cusp*, it implies a pull towards airy, intellectual, logical unions and sometimes towards partners with air signs — i.e. Gemini, Libra, Aquarius — dominating their charts. Often, too, because air blows easily this way and that, the risk of taking permanent involvements too lightly, seeking the blending of like minds while forgetting that like bodily needs are equally important.

If one of your parents was an air sign type *and* greatly affected your ideas about marriage, you will often find that parent's sign or element on your 7th house cusp.

● *The plus* with air here is that it is capable of promoting lightness and intellectual stimulation in long-term relationships.
● *The minus* with air here is that it is equally capable of blowing them away.

When you spot an *earth sign on the 7th house cusp*, it implies a pull towards earthy, dependable, realistic unions and sometimes towards partners with earth signs — i.e. Taurus, Virgo, Capricorn — dominating their charts. Often, too, because earth is hard and stony, the risk of seeking heavy permanent involvements that are functional but demanding.

If one of your parents was an earth sign type *and* greatly affected your ideas about marriage, you will often find that parent's sign or element on your 7th house cusp.

● *The plus* with earth here is that it is capable of promoting strength and supportiveness in long-term relationships.
● *The minus* with earth here is that it is equally capable of bogging them down.

When you spot a *water sign on the 7th house cusp*, it implies a pull towards watery, emotional, fluid unions and sometimes towards partners with water signs — i.e. Cancer, Scorpio, Pisces — dominating their charts. Often, too, because water is capable of dragging everything down into its eddying depths, the risk of seeking unstable permanent involvements that are far too subject to moods and undercurrents.

If one of your parents was a water sign type *and* greatly affected your ideas about marriage, you will often find that parent's sign or element on your 7th house cusp.

● *The plus* with water here is that it is capable of promoting depths and sensitivity in long-term relationships.
● *The minus* with water here is that it is equally capable of drowning them.

Testing your Findings

Gather together now all the charts you have — partners, lovers, family, friends — and check what you know about their lives against the chart indicators we've been discussing up to this point. Then compile your own set of statistics. I have done just that as part of my own research programme for more than ten years and found that people do obey the dictates of their charts far too often for it to be chance or coincidence. You will observe it too.

As an added test of skill, try working on compatibility anlayses for famous lovers/married couples. Birth data can usually be located in encyclopaedias and other works of reference. Most good astrology bookshops also stock books of prepared charts of famous individuals from Julius Caesar to John Lennon.

For example: Why *did* Napoleon marry Josephine when he obviously did not love her? Why *did* Hitler spend his leisure hours with a girl as simple as Eva Braun? What *was* the story with U.S. President John Kennedy and wife Jackie?

Choose famous pairs who interest you and check out your findings. This exercise will not only polish your skill and prove many of the pointers we've been discussing but also teach you to view charts with greater detachment. It's not all that easy to be detached about the personality pros and cons of those closest to you, but in expert analysis detachment is vital.

Seventh House Planets: The Relationships They Promise

Now, let's adjust our microscopes for a closer look at the 7th house by listing the planets occupying it with particular reference to potential compatibility. Don't forget, of course, that some charts show *empty 7th houses*. This does *not* mean their owners will never marry or make a lasting commitment. In my experiences, an empty 7th points to the fact that this individual is far less likely to use marriage — consciously or unconsciously — as a means of learning and evolving. Union is not a reigning need in the personality.

What happens when you see *more than one planet* or even several in the 7th house? Immediately, we observe massive emphasis placed on the house (or life sector) which the group occupies. The emphasis is heavier still if the house in question is an angle, i.e. 1st, 4th, 7th, 10th, and heavier still again if the group comprises five or more planets, termed a 'stellium' or 'satellitium'.

The individual whose chart contains a stellium — and in my experience, even three planets are often enough — is inexorably drawn to express himself/herself in that life sector. Thus, where this kind of emphasis focuses on the 7th house, the individual is literally dragged into relationships by the hair of the head. The urge to unite, to blend is so relentless, there's no final escape from it. However, depending on other chart indicators — and especially when a heavy like Pluto is in the 7th — attempts are often made, consciously or unconsciously, earlier in the life to evade commitment. Why? Because the individual knows instinctively how much will be demanded of him/her. They may try to dodge out from under but, like the long arm of the law, a strong 7th always catches its quarry in the end.

In any event, whenever you find more than one planet in any house of the horoscope chart you must allow for the effects of two separate and possibly conflicting energies on the affairs of that house.

Let's say you're looking at pleasing, peace-loving Venus sitting next to wild, freedom-loving Uranus in the 7th house. Many other factors in the chart must as ever be tied in with this placement but it does presage a strange mixture of self-will and romanticism. Charismatic appeal? Certainly. Predictable? Never.

As we'll observe now the planets found in the 7th house reveal in their various ways the likely behaviour in permanent relationships of their 'owners'. Bear in mind, of course, that such planetary influences rarely manifest in any obvious manner in the early days of courtship or co-habitation.

This fact is especially noticeable with all the 'heavies', i.e. Saturn, Uranus, Neptune and Pluto. Their effects may take a long time to surface in overt behaviour. Sometimes they will lie low for years, awaiting an event or confrontation that will light the fuse.

Another concealing agent — which we'll discuss in detail in Chapter 5 — is the Ascendant, which often acts as a mask, assumed to hide the true personality. Since the Ascendant shows how each individual *wishes* to be seen by others, it takes a very long time — even when couples are together twenty-four hours a day — before the mask is dropped.

One last point (before we look at planets aspecting each other from the 7th house) is this. You may be wondering why people born under signs ruled by 7th house planets sometimes appear in the life as rivals. At first surprisingly, but not when you think about it, the 7th house has been regarded also as 'the house of open enemies' from early in the history of astrology. This secondary meaning becomes clearer if we look back at previous paragraphs in this section and recall that many of our immature and egotistical demands have to be forsworn if we desire total union with another. So, in a sense, partnership is the enemy of egocentricity. 'Me-first' has to give way to 'us-first' — but sometimes not without a fight!

Seventh House Data at a Glance

The focus on the 7th	Reveals all kinds of liaisons throughout adult life; type of partner attracted or desired; ease or lack of it in relating.

The planets in the 7th   Add further emphasis on the above; help or hinder conjugal harmony; introduce cooperative or separative behaviour.

The aspects to the 7th   Link up other houses with marriage/union; easy aspects promise assistance from activities in other life areas; awkward aspects threaten direction of energies away from marital responsibilities.

Sun in the 7th: Solar view of marriage/unions, i.e. search for warmth, brightness. Directs the will towards formation of long-term relationships. Desire is to shine: choice of mate partially dictated by his/her ability to impress others. May adopt a commanding, I'm-always-right stance in arguments. Subconscious fear of domination possible. May be attracted to but also find rivalry with anyone who has the sign of Leo prominent.

Moon in the 7th: Lunar view of marriage/unions, i.e. search for softness, sensitivity. Directs the emotions towards fulfilment in long-term relationships. Desire is to reflect: choice of mate partially dictated by his/her capacity to elicit right response. May adopt a moody, don't-touch-me stance in arguments. Indecision about final commitment possible. May be attracted to but also find rivalry with anyone who has the sign of Cancer prominent.

Mercury in the 7th: Mercurial view of marriage/unions, i.e. search for intellectual stimulation, quick perception. Directs the mind towards mental compatibility in long-term relationships. Desire is to communicate: choice of mate partially dictated by his/her ability to exchange ideas. May adopt bickering, I'm-smarter-than-you stance. Easily bored by slow-thinking, long-winded reactions. May be attracted to but also find rivalry with anyone who has the signs of Gemini or Virgo prominent.

Venus in the 7th: Venusian view of marriage/unions, i.e. search for harmony, companionship. Directs the affections towards grace and pleasantness in long-term relationships. Desire is to please: choice of mate partially dictated by his/her good looks and personal charms. May adopt a vacillating, peace-at-any-price stance in arguments. Concern with appearances rather than realities possible. May be attracted to but also find rivalry with anyone who has the signs of Taurus or Libra prominent.

Mars in the 7th: Martian view of marriage/unions; i.e. search for passion, excitement. Directs the sexual drives towards combat and vitality in long-term relationships. Desire is to arouse: choice of mate partially dictated by his/her physical vigour and obvious sexuality. May adopt a truculent, chip-on-the-shoulder stance in arguments. Pugnacity, impatience possible. May be attracted to but also find rivalry with anyone who has the signs of Aries or Scorpio prominent.

Jupiter in the 7th: Jupiterian view of marriage/unions; i.e. search for optimism and generosity. Directs the opportunistic instincts towards advancement of status through long-term relationships. Desire is to expand: choice of mate partially dictated by his/her personal prestige and social standing. May adopt an improvident, trust-to-luck stance. Extravagance, over-confidence possible. May be attracted to but also find rivalry with anyone who has the sign of Sagittarius prominent.

Saturn in the 7th: Saturnian view of marriage/unions; i.e. search for loyalty, responsibility. Directs the ambitions towards establishment of stable, serious long-term relationships. Desire is to control: choice of mate partially dictated by his/her willingness to accept direction. May adopt a dogmatic, nobody-appreciates-me stance. Austerity, contempt for non-achievers possible. May be attracted to but also find rivalry with anyone who has the sign of Capricorn prominent.

Uranus in the 7th: Uranian view of marriage/unions, i.e. search for freedom, independence. Directs the progressive instincts towards unconventionality and lack of restriction in long-term relationships. Desire is to electrify: choice of mate partially dictated by his/her unorthodoxy and originality. May adopt a rebellious, I've-got-to-be-me stance in arguments. Over-detachment, wilfulness possible. May be attracted to but also find rivalry with anyone who has the sign of Aquarius prominent.

Neptune in the 7th: Neptunian view of marriage/unions; i.e. search for inspiration, spirituality. Directs the idealistic urges towards subtlety and sentimentality in long-term relationships. Desire is to merge: choice of mate partially dictated by his/her gentleness and sensitivity. May adopt a nebulous, head-in-the-clouds stance. Fantasizing, self-deception possible. May be attracted to but also find rivalry with anyone who has the sign of Pisces prominent.

Pluto in the 7th: Plutonian view of marriage/unions, i.e. search for regeneration, revelations. Directs the subconscious drives towards power struggles and intensity in long-term relationships. Desire is to dominate: choice of mate partially dictated by his/her inner reserves and resilience. May adopt an uncooperative, my-way-or-else stance. Outpourings of resentment and provocative behaviour possible. May be attracted to but also find rivalry with anyone who has the sign of Scorpio prominent.

Aspects to the Seventh: Further Compatibilty Clues

Just a quick reminder as to the interrelated roles played by the planets in determining human responses before we discuss the aspects themselves. Always keep in mind that:

- Each planet symbolizes a specific *principle* (or fundamental source) of behaviour.
- The sign in which each planet appears indicates the specific *manner* in which such principle will reveal itself.
- The house which each planet occupies points to the specific life *area* where such influence will be most clearly seen.

Now you're ready to begin assessing planetary aspects for yourself and your partner, check over if necessary the same steps set out in Chapter 2.

Marriage House Aspects — Check-List

Since planetary aspects involving the 7th house are of particular value in assessing conjugal compatibility as regards similar or conflicting attitudes to marriage, we'll list hereunder in-brief interpretations of some of the more common aspects to offer guide-lines.

- In own chart, easy aspects, i.e. some conjunctions, trines and sextiles, improve prospects of successful union.
- In cross-referenced man-to-woman charts, easy aspects between own and partner's planets promise even better prospects.
- Awkward aspects, i.e. some conjunctions, squares and oppositions, have a deleterious effect and imply incompatible behaviour.
- Predominance of easy aspects obviously makes for more comfortable

relationships *but* predominance of awkward aspects does not threaten disaster. Here, much greater effort has to be expended *by both partners,* however, to make the union workable.

Sun to Moon (Will and Emotions)
Easy Aspects = Own chart — added harmony within the self;
              = Man/Woman charts — better acceptance of each other.
Hard Aspects = Exact reversal of above.

Sun to Venus (Will and Affections)
Easy Aspects = Own chart — added personal charm;
              = Man/Woman charts — uncomplicated exchange of affection.
Hard Aspects = Exact reversal of above.

Sun to Mars (Will and Sex Drives)
Easy Aspects = Own chart — added physical vitality;
              = Man/Woman charts — intensification of passion.
Hard Aspects = Exact reverse of above.

Moon to Venus (Emotions and Affections)
Easy Aspects = Own chart — added emotional equilibruim;
              = Man/Woman charts — increased warmth of feeling.
Hard Aspects = Exact reverse of above.

Moon to Mars (Emotions and Sex Drives)
Easy Aspects = Own chart — added spontaneity in displaying passion;
              = Man/Woman charts — better understanding of each other's sexual needs.
 Hard Aspects = Exact reverse of above.

Moon to Saturn (Emotions and Discipline)
Easy Aspects = Own chart — added sense of duty and responsibility;
              = Man/Woman charts — better capacity for faithfulness and stability in union.
Hard Aspects = Exact reverse of above.

Mercury to Mars (Mentality and Vitality)
Easy Aspects = Own chart — added speed and vigour in thinking;
              = Man/Woman charts — better capacity to offer mental stimulation to each other.

Hard Aspects = Exact reverse of above.

Venus to Mars (Affections and Passions)
Easy Aspects = Own chart — added capacity to blend feelings and physical desires;
= Man/Woman charts — better ability to mix affection with sexual activity.
Hard Aspects = Exact reverse of above.

Venus to Jupiter (Affections and Opportunities)
Easy Aspects = Own chart — added capacity to offer and attract generosity;
= Man/Woman charts — better ability to share gains willingly.
Hard Aspects = Exact reverse of above.

Venus to Saturn (Affections and Discipline)
Easy Aspects = Own chart — added capacity for steady, supportive affection;
= Man/Woman charts — better ability to apply self-control and forbearance.
Hard Aspects = Exact reverse of above.

Heavy Planets (Uranus, Neptune and Pluto)
Although when personal planets make aspects to one or more of these three, behavioural responses are notably affected in the individual chart, their effect on cross-referenced aspects in man/woman charts is of lesser significance.

Once again, the list of these possible aspects is too numerous to repeat here so if you're not already familiar with them, you'll find all described in my companion book *How to Astro-Analyse Yourself and Others* or in any other authoritative astrological text.

At this stage, we're considering planetary aspects with special reference to their effect on behaviour in marriage/union situations, so let's put our plan into action with an example.

Planetary 'Conversations'

Imagine you're looking at a chart which exhibits the following aspects.

A doubting, depriving 1st house Saturn stares stonily out across the chart at the dark, inscrutable face of Pluto in the 7th. The aspect is an opposition. Fear (Saturn) and Fate (Pluto) confront each other. The individual wavers — caught between two massive and uncompromising energy fields. Anxieties multiply when the aspect is triggered by events. Obsessions thrust upwards from the subconscious.

What to do? Which way to go? Stay hiding away alone behind the protective wall Saturn has painstakingly built up around the self? Or run into the waiting but nonetheless frightening arms of the partner Pluto has chosen?

The dilemma is instinctively felt, rarely consciously thought over — as if the two planets were engaging in conversations heard only by the inner ear:

'You must marry. You must take the one I offer you. It is your destiny', whispers Pluto.

'Don't trust him,' Saturn counters at once. 'He will destroy you. Stay with me where you're safe'.

'Of course, I will destroy you,' agrees Pluto. 'Through marriage, I will destroy the person you thought yourself to be so you can be transformed. A Phoenix rising from the ashes of egotism'.

'Ashes are right,' growls Saturn. 'He's into ashes. *I* am the Lord of the World. I can give you everything the world offers if you listen to me'.

'Ah, yes. The World'. Pluto sounds reflective. 'He always promises that when he's up against me. His glum little world, filled with its narrow little ambitions. Take it and — in the end — you'll see which of us was offering you ashes'.

The Saturn/Pluto opposition when it links up the 1st and 7th houses is a particularly tough one. That is why I chose it and dramatized it to emphasize the tremendous force of major planetary aspects on reactions to vital decisions in everyone's life, of which marriage is undoubtedly one.

However, we need to consider much more than whatever aspects are affecting marital compatibility, so we'll now resume the continuing story of our specimen couple — Harry and Helen.

1. *7th house cusp:*
    Harry has an earth sign there; Helen has an air sign. Harry is a

markedly air type; Helen is a markedly earth type. So far, so good. Here at least they both obeyed the pull of their charts. He instinctively sought an earthy, realistic partner, who would set marriage on a practical basis. She instinctively sought an airy, intellectually able partner, who would set the marriage on a communicative basis.

2. *Planets in 7th:*

   Harry's 7th house is empty. So marriage is not an area where he feels driven to perform. Helen has Pluto there. Trouble again! She's uncharacteristically intense when it comes to union, forced to change her basic personality structure through a husband. Harry doesn't want that job, yet the demand gets through to him. He feels pressurized, adopting a dominating stance to compensate. The power struggles begin.

3. *Aspects to the 7th:*

   Harry doesn't have any. Helen's Pluto has a mixed bag, linking up the 11th house (Hopes & Wishes, Love Received) and the 4th (Home, Domestic Conditions). Resentment grows, spreading round Helen's chart. His definition of love/marriage is not hers. Her hopes and longings are alien to him. She presses for solutions. He doesn't know what's bugging her. It's all too heavy.

When we mix these additional pointers in with those which emerged from this pair's 4th house indicators, we can see the rocks and potholes along the marital road are stacking up more ominously.

Now, as in Chapter 2, blend in the new data we've gathered in your own charts as we've just done with Harry and Helen. Is the picture brighter or darker? Are there cupids ready to flutter round the breakfast table? Or have they suddenly acquired horns and tails?

If the latter, step warily. Both of you will need to make a greater effort to tie together securely two packages of contrary needs and expectations.

Nevertheless, incompatible 7th house pictures do not deny successful union and much can be learned from living with them. From viewing our own faults through the eyes of a partner, we gain a new perspective of ourselves. Often the view is less than flattering but invariably enlightening.

Five Certain Marriage-Wreckers —
and How to Spot Them

Many years ago when I practised as a lawyer, I spent a large portion of time advising divorce petitioners. And, as I did so, I applied my psychological and astrological training to research the reasons why each marriage had gone off the rails. I found there were a number of recurring themes — types of conduct which are virtually guaranteed to drive the spouse to drink, desperation and divorce. Sadly, the perpetrators were often consciously unaware of how relentlessly they were driving nails into the coffin of love each time they acted as they did. Sadder still, their behaviour invariably sparked off retaliatory action in their partners, ranging from sarcasm to sexual impotence, from workaholism to chronic depression.

Indeed, it is an illuminating and alarming experience to read affidavits by divorcing partners as to what went on in their failed marriages. Self-delusion, deception, repressed anger, self-justification, fantasies often underly every phrase in such documents, indicating how sparse was the knowledge each party had gained of the other in years upon years of marriage. Sometimes the two accounts were so wildly disparate, you kept looking at the title of the documents to ensure you really were reading about the lives of the same couple.

Yet, in every case, I found that by merely checking their astrological patterns on the day of birth, anyone trained in astro-analysis could pinpoint where the seeds of marital discord were most likely to sprout. If the participants in a broken or breaking marriage had been alerted to these *before* they went to the altar, they may have decided to forget the whole thing, or have been more prepared to tolerate each other's shortcomings.

There is no doubt that some individuals are not psychologically equipped to meet the demands of permanent union. But they are the exception, not the rule, Most of us can handle relationships and make them work better *if* we try.

So let's consider the worst in a long list of marriage-wrecking attitudes for the purpose of watching for them in our own behaviour as well as our partner's.

As you'll observe, all are highly negative and hence extremely destructive to both partners at a deeply subconscious level. That's why it is important to think about each one carefully without saying to yourself: 'Oh, *I* don't do that sort of thing!'

As Freud and many other of the great psychoanalysts pointed out, the conscious mind sets up blocks which allow us to rationalize or justify undesirable behaviour, at the same time repressing awareness of its underlying motivation. The truth *will* out, however. I well remember two separate male clients who wrote to me about their problems. Both used the same sentence: 'At present, I'm having serious martial troubles!' No, that was *not* a spelling error. The conscious mind clearly intended to say 'marital troubles' but the subconscious mind slyly slipped in the truth. This is what is psychologically termed a 'Freudian slip'. Both men were subconsciously viewing their marriages as a battlefield. And, their charts showed that's exactly what the relationship was.

As you'll note with the following list of marriage-wrecking attitudes, I've described them in lighter vein to make for easier reading, but that definitely does not mean they should be taken lightly.

Some individuals show traces of several such attitudes. Few of us are saintly enough, if we're brutally honest with ourselves, to claim we've never exhibited one or other of them.

1. The Bedside Reformer Attitude

This one turns marriage into a life sentence in a corrective institution. A list of all partner's sins requiring reform is kept handy on what amounts to a mental 'bedside table'.

Spoken statements go like this: 'I'm doing everything I can to help you make the most of yourself!'

Unspoken statements go like this: 'You're a walking disaster area! I'll show the world what a sterling character *I* am by teaching you the error of your ways.

Result: Break-up at worst; smouldering resentment at best here. The time for training human personality ended in childhood so the would-be reformer is light-years too late. And who gave Partner A the divine right to decide what's wrong with Partner B anyway?

Astro-clues: Any chart indicator stressing over-disciplinary, authoritative behaviour: equally those implying subconscious desire to punish whoever does not conform to high but narrow standards. A harsh Saturn also often has a hand in the 'Bedside Reformer' attitude as do signs stimulating oppressive, dominating traits.

2. The Altar Urger Attitude

This one thinks of wedding bells at the blink of an interested eye. The march to the altar turns into a sprint.

Spoken Statements go like this: 'It was love at first sight, wasn't it? Let's get married tomorrow!'

Unspoken Statements go like this: 'If I don't get a ring on to this one fast, I might be left in the lurch again!'

Result: Rude awakening here. Each partner is marrying a total stranger whose party manners haven't had time to slip. When continued intimacy breaks through them, the true personality beneath may be horrendously incompatible. Whirlwind marriages based on brief acquaintances allow no cooling-off period between the thought of the marriage contract and its signature.

Astro-Clues: Any chart indicator promoting reckless or ill-considered behaviour: equally those implying subconscious fear of rejection. A hot-blooded Mars or mad-headed Uranus also often trigger the 'Altar Urger' attitude as do signs stimulating lack of forethought and impetuosity.

3. The Meal Ticket Collector Attitude

This one looks at marriage as a business investment, toting up financial assets and liabilities with the detail of a computerized accountant.

Spoken statements go like this: 'I always say anyone who thinks two can live as cheaply as one is just plain silly!'

Unspoken statements go like this: 'You look like a going concern. Somebody's got to support me because I can't (or won't) do it myself!'

Result: A using situation here. Too one-sided, too cold-blooded. Arguments about money quickly rip apart whatever remnants of genuine feeling may exist.

Astro clues: Any chart indicator which suggests emotional security is equated with financial security: equally those which infer continuing sense of personal inadequacy.

A fearful Saturn or an irresponsible Neptune also often underly the 'Meal Ticket Collector' attitude as do signs stressing laziness or lack of drive.

4. The One-Upmanship Attitude
This one is into keeping up with the proverbial Joneses. Other people's households are viewed as competing images of success.

Spoken statements go like this: 'It's only natural to want the best for your family!'

Unspoken statements go like this: 'I measure personal worth in money. If you can't give me more than our neighbours have, you're not worth a cracker!'

Result: A pressure-building situation here. Overstress on material gain with love tied to the wallet. Placating the demand for constant spending only brings further demand. Partner on receiving end of this barrage will have to go broke or get out.

Astro-clues: Any chart indicator stressing misdirected competitive drives or plain, old-fashioned avarice: equally those which infer obsessive urge to acquire and show off.

A competitive Mars, an improvident Jupiter or a compulsive Pluto also often stir up the 'One-Upmanship' attitude as do signs generating over-expansiveness and vanity.

5. The Finders-Keepers Attitude
This one works on the principle that once a partner is found, he or she'll be kept for ever, no matter what is served up to them. Sloppy habits, plain bad manners, ill temper are expected to be taken as part of the deal.

Spoken statements go like this: 'If you can't be yourself in your own home, where can you?'

Unspoken statements go like this: 'Now that I've got you where I want you, to hell with frills. You're not worth taking any trouble for anyway!'

Result: Double damage here. Both partners end up as 'losers-weepers'. The don't-care partner creates a retaliatory don't-care response in the other. Both feel undermined, unappreciated.

Astro-clues: Any chart indicator stressing self-indulgence, lack of discipline, dislike of self.

A negative Neptune, an inhibited Mars or repressive Pluto also engender the 'Finders-Keepers' attitude as do signs promoting suppressed anger and idleness.

So there they are in all their glory. Five easy ways to wreck a marriage or ruin a relationship.

In each, you'll observe a strong undercurrent of self-deception and self-justification . . . those camouflaging devices the conscious mind employs to make destructive behaviour *appear* proper.

If you spot the beginnings of any of them in your own reactions, make a resolution now to dig them out. If you spot them in a prospective lover, look before you leap into partnership.

Quick reference check-points
Plus or Minus Indicators of Marital Expectations

Opposites do attract: Psychologically, you will often find yourself attracted to partner whose personality traits are the precise opposite of your own; e.g. introverts may go for extroverts and vice versa. Astrologically, this pull is shown by oppositions in own chart and cross-referenced man/woman charts; e.g. strongly Leonine types may fall for strongly Aquarian types. This kind of attraction is often intense, but with it comes recurring and equally intense irritation, caused by irreconcilable differences. Thus when it happens, you need to 'Handle With Care!'

Sun spotting: Ancient astrology texts assert the position of the Sun in a female chart will imply early or late marriage; i.e. before or after the age of 30. Sun in 4th, 5th, 6th, 10th, 11th or 12th houses is held to show permanent union in the first years of adult life. Sun in 1st, 2nd, 3rd, 7th, 8th or 9 th houses either delays marriage or suggests choice of a very much older mate.

Personally, I have found this theory is not infallible, but it often works and thus is worth checking.

Mating with the same mistake: It is alarmingly common to find individuals teaming up again and again with exact prototypes of the first unsatisfactory partner. Sometimes the new mate is even a perfect look-alike of the previous one too! Attraction to a specific type of looks and personality is shown by the chart. One of my female clients, a strongly Libran type, worked her way through no less than four disastrous unions with strongly Cancerian males before she understood how to redirect her natal chart patterns — *and* steer clear of Cancer-style trouble!

One or many: Double-bodied signs on the 7th house cusp often predispose towards more than one, even several marriages/unions. These signs are Gemini, symbolized by the twin youths; Sagittarius, symbolized by the half-human, half-horse figure of the centaur; and Pisces, symbolized by the bound-together pair of fish. All are mutable signs, thus indicating changeful attitudes to marriage and desire for variety in partners.

May-Decembers: Whereas in earlier times, May-December matings usually meant a much older man and a young woman, nowadays there is a growing tendency for older women to choose young men as permanent partners. Either way much additional care is needed to make such relationships endure against the onslaught of time. Three danger spots to be watched are:

1. Differing generation planets;
2. Variable intensity of sexual needs;
3. Desire, or lack of it, for children.

The first suggests quite different 'gut reactions' as to definition of marriage and its obligations. The second suggests problems if the younger partner is highly sexed. Venus and Mars especially reveal this. The third arises since older mates may not want children, have had them already or be physically incapable of producing them. Attitudes towards offspring are shown by each chart. These are fully discussed in the next chapter. Plainly, however, if your chart demands children and your partner blocks this need, clashes must ensue.

Marrying 'Mum' or 'Dad': Some psychoanalysts maintain we all marry or team up with the person who most resembles our mothers. Not physically, of course but in temperament and behaviour because as infants we learnt from her what love and affection were and weren't meant to be. Personally, I consider there is much truth in this statement although I would never discount the father's role in directing partner choices at the subconscious level. Countless individuals do select a mate of the same sign as one of the parents or with very similar chart patterns. Problems with this choice were fully discussed in Chapter 2.

Male v. female: Despite wildly oscillating lifestyles, trends and sexual roles in the Age of Aquarius, the ancient battle of the sexes must end not in conquest of one by the other but in a truce. The biological nature and temperament of the male as compared to the female is as different and as clear-cut in the human species as it is in all other animals. The difference is so fundamental that (as astrological author Martin Pentecost pointed out) archaeologists can decide from the inspection of a single tooth dug up from campsites of pre-historic man whether the owner was male or female!

Thus when comparing charts of existing or intending partners, bear this in mind. I do not believe interpretations of aspects and other chart indicators should be varied in any material way when the subject is a man or woman. However, when you think about them, remember they will be expressed *in a male or female way*.

Second time around: It is all too common in new unions to blame the new partner for the faults and shortcomings of his/her predecessor. The more so if a great deal of hurt and damage to your own self-image has lingered on. We all have far too many faults of our own to handle without being lumbered with those belonging to somebody else. If a chart shows the inclination to brood over the past, to seek revenge for long-ago wrongs, or to set overly steep standards, this problem can occur, although it may not be consciously realized. These are cases where great effort must be made to toss ancient history onto the marital scrap-heap.

Now, we've worked our way through the rocky ifs and buts, the thorny pros and cons in the state of matrimony or its equivalent, we can uphold the truth of the old maxim: 'Marriages are made in Heaven.'

The map of the heavens at the moment of birth shows the path we must tread as plainly as a street directory. But, to quote another maxim: 'God helps those who help themselves.' Hence we can use our own free will to skirt the quagmires of misery, to apply tolerance and understanding along the road finally to arrive at that most coveted of all human destinations — a truly happy marriage. However, this point is not the end of the story. We must now turn our attention to the 5th house and decide what part romantic hopes and children play in the life drama.

CHAPTER FOUR

The Pursuit of Love — Winning or Losing?

Definitions of Love

What *is* this thing called love? This mix of overwhelming emotion, consuming desire and endless longing? That can strike with the blinding flash of Uranian lightning, blasting us to the stars when reciprocated or burning us to ashes when spurned? That can forge bonds so strong they stretch beyond the grave? Or so fragile they break in a moment?

From the time Man discovered he could write, he has been trying to trap love in words. To explain why it happens. To define exactly what it is. Without any noticeable success. For love, like happiness means different things to different people. And in any event, there are so many varieties of it. In this chapter, we're only trying to understand one — i.e. what is called 'romantic' love, for want of a better adjective: love between a man and a woman.

That, too, is far from easy to pin down psychologically, since you must try to untangle a positive mare's nest of emotions, drives, needs and fantasies, many of which contradict each other — but somehow manage to weave themselves together in the subconscious mind and finally surface as love. In a sense, it's rather like trying to catch a butterfly with a mousetrap! Human intellectual equipment is too cumbersome to grasp hold of something which constantly flits away, changing colour and direction before your very eyes.

Even if you take a pair of true lovers for laboratory specimens — as it were — and plot their joint progress through life from youth's passions all the way to age's calm happiness in each other, neither psychiatry nor psychoanalysis can supply answers to all the 'hows' and 'whys'. For this thing called love, when the genuine article, changes and transmutes itself from what it was when it began to what it finally becomes in many and mysterious ways. And yet, in its very essence, it remains the same. Thus, deciding what love actually *is* adds up to a tough assignment!

Still, we must at least attempt to define it because if we don't really know what love is, we won't know what we're searching for with the aid of the astro-analytical data set out in this chapter.

Perhaps, the only uncomplicated statement to be made about it is:

Once found, love will light up your life. Once lost, love can black out your life, sometimes for ever.

Obviously then, the pursuit of love is a perilous undertaking yet the desire to love and be loved is so deeply-rooted in the human psyche few indeed refuse to join in the chase. So we need all the help we can get. In seeking out love. In sorting the sheep from the goats, the brief infatuations or sexual turn-ons from 'the real, real thing'.

As ever, astro-analysis will throw us a life-belt when we look like drowning in a sea of troubles. By showing who is right and who is wrong for us, what we want of love and what we're likely to get — via, among other things, the 5th house of the horoscope chart.

But before we venture deeper into the territory of the 5th, let's cast another glance at Venus and Mars, the planets named after the ancient deities of love and war.

In the horoscope chart, this pair in particular preside over all kinds of attractions between male and female, promising happiness or disappointment, sexual fulfilment or frustration according to their signs, house positions and aspects.

Perhaps, you wonder how Mars, the fiery war god, got himself astrologically involved in love affairs. The choice becomes less surprising when you remember that Mars symbolizes the sexual side of love. And in many ways, there is a suggestion of the violent in all sexual activity as witness the quite savage grimace of the human face during orgasm. The desperate clutching, the loud cries, the thrusting of one body against the other.

Such a vision is a long step indeed from the affectionate side of love which Venus symbolizes — the soft words, the gentle caresses, the joyful smiles. Yet sex remains an integral part of romantic love.

If you're a normal human being and you love someone in the romantic sense, you want to go to bed with that person. Nevertheless, at the beginning of a relationship it is sometimes very, very difficult to know for certain whether what you're feeling is in fact love or merely sexual desire.

That question is far more complicated than it sounds at first — so complicated indeed that world-famous psychoanalyst Dr Theodor Reik devoted his massive 623 page book entitled *Of Love and Lust* to examining its ramifications.

To help us solve the problem as to what our true feelings are, Dr Reik lists numerous findings that are well worth reflecting upon — especially if you already believe you love someone or are about to take the plunge into a new relationship. I'll list some of his more salient comparisons between love and sexual attraction below:

'The sex urge hunts for lustful pleasure. Love is in search of joy and happiness.'

'You can force another person to sexual activity but not to love.'

'Sex is a passionate interest in another body; love a passionate interest in another personality, or his life.'

'Sex can be casual about its object. Love cannot. Love is always a personal relationship.'

'The object of sex may become of no account, boring or even hateful immediately after satisfaction is reached. Not so the love object.'

'Sex is undiscriminating, selfish and in extreme cases, utterly selfish. Love is highly discriminating and it is very difficult to name its selfish aims, other than that of being happy in the happiness of the beloved person.'

Thus in even these few quotes, you can begin to see the huge differences which exist between the feeling of love and the urge of sex. You can see why it is possible to feel sexual desire for a specific individual intensely and over long periods *without* ever coming to love that person.

You can perceive the origin of the anguish every woman feels when a man offers love in words but denies it by his actions, by showing disinterest or even outright dislike once sexual intercourse is over. Nevertheless, I rather doubt that it is possible to love someone in the romantic sense *without* sexually desiring that person. (The only noticeable exceptions to that rule are cases of lovers who've grown very old together. The sexual urge has by then died but love is as alive as ever.)

Still, to put it in astrological terms, you're running into trouble if you try to divorce Venus from her natural consort, Mars!

As I have pointed out many times before in my books, astrology, like all sciences, is a language of symbols. The more clearly you are able to understand the symbols, the greater your skill in using them becomes. The astrological symbolism of the marriage of Venus and Mars (the union of love and sex) is crystallized in those ancient myths which narrate how Zeus, chief of the Olympian gods, found (despite numerous attempts and assorted commands) he could not marry the love goddess Venus off to anyone else *but* Mars. There were other suitor deities, patently better husband material than that epitome of macho maleness — the swaggering, red-cloaked, sword-brandishing war god. But Venus flatly refused to stay with any of them. Thereby she proclaimed for all time that love and its sexual expression belong together.

The exploration of long-lived myths in the analysis of human behaviour is not in any sense whatsoever a retreat into mysticism, magic or superstition. As the leading Jungian analyst, Edward C. Whitmont, M.D., explains in his brilliantly researched book *The Symbolic Quest*, there is an astonishing similarity in the story line of myths, preserved over centuries and emanating from widely differing cultures throughout the world. The heroes and gods have different names and wear different apparel but the tales are basically the same. How did this happen? Because myths illustrate in a simple narrative form that could always be understood by everyone (like parables), the strongest and most urgent human needs and desires, two of which are love and sex. These needs have always been present and remain virtually unchanged since Man evolved into a thinking, striving animal.

Thus the story and the symbolism behind the union of Venus (love/affection) and Mars (sex/physical drives) have to be borne in mind constantly when equating — from the standpoint of astro-analysis — the precise capacities and expectations of every pair of lovers.

Before we go any further, take a detailed look at all the pointers relating to Venus and Mars in your own chart and your partner's.

1.   Consider the elemental stress as set out in Chapter 2.
2.   Visualize the signs of Venus and Mars.
3.   Examine their aspects, wherever the planets are located in the chart.
4.   Blend in the early home conditioning as set out in Chapter 4.

5.   Check for contradictions or confirmations of attitudes generated by all the foregoing factors.

This exercise will throw greater light on potential compatibility or lack of it. Don't rush through this step. Think about it calmly and carefully. Keep in mind the fact that, while no analyst would advise long-term union between partners that were sexually incompatible and thus unable to satisfy each other, nobody spends all his/her time in a clinch. That is why astrological data revealing the many other facets of the personalities of the two lovers has to be meticulously compared.

Sadly, love does *not* conquer all things — at least not permanently, although, if you've just fallen madly for the most perfect human being who ever walked this earth, you won't be in the mood to believe that. Personality clashes, even trivial habits, are capable of destroying love. Sexual attraction is adept at disguising itself as love. This last is particularly true of the extravagantly passionate variety, immortalized in the tragic tale of Romeo and Juliet. But *was* that love? Both were little more than children, who had barely set eyes on each other. Rebuffed by a previous girl, Romeo was on the rebound — still a common reason for falling instantly 'in love'. Add to all that two sets of actively feuding in-laws, who ran each other through with a sword and without a qualm, and you'd have to admit you have the worst possible scenario for future conjugal bliss.

More than likely — and is so often the case with sudden, intense attractions — theirs was not 'love at first sight' but 'lust at first sight'! Shakespeare was well aware of this and wisely killed his young lovers off before Romeo had a chance to come home late and complain about his dinner, or Juliet told him where to go because one of the children was screaming or his second cousin had just written off her favourite uncle.

Stories like Romeo and Juliet survive because most of us would like to imagine true love is all passionate adoration on the peaks of ecstasy. But it is not. True love is living together happily through what another poet once called 'the long littleness of life'. The everyday.

Shakespeare himself was a down-to-earth Taurean, blessed with an unerring knowledge of human psychology. Thus he clearly understood the flaming passions which characterize the early days of intense attraction cannot possibly survive for long. And may not, in fact, be love at all.

To begin with, it's much too much. It literally burns the couple out because rash, mad-headed, impetutous Mars is at the controls. The sensations are exhausting, fevered, fluctuating between ecstasy and anguish. You can't sleep, can't think, can't eat, barely exist unless the 'beloved' is there beside you.

Alas, when the party's over — and no matter how wild and wonderful, it must end — you wake up to look upon your partner in the grim light of a morning after. That's when the crunch comes and you discover whether it *was* merely Mars who got you into this or whether Venus is still around somewhere.

Curiously, in this Aquarian age of advanced technology and universal education (which means we *ought* to know better), we are even more inclined to mistake sexual desire for love than our less sophisticated forbears were in Shakespeare's day. This is due to the fact that present-day advertising sells sexual fantasies, frequently disguised as love, to sell *things*. Virtually anything. Images of beautiful people, doing exciting things together or looking as if they're just about to make beautiful love to each other, flicker endlessly across our television screens.

Nobody 'in love' is ever plain, fat, ordinary, old or short of money as real people are in the real world. Moreover, beneath the glossy surface, a message comes through loud and clear. This informs us that the only things of value in life are those which are superficially and visibly attractive. Youth and physical beauty. The good life in its purely materialistic sense. By these means we can be persuaded to try to buy a better shape, a youthful face, more hair, another whatever. And, conversely, the message implies that kindness, intelligence, understanding are without real worth because such qualities have no commercial value.

Day and night pretty television brides (who've craftily used the right perfume) float towards the altar on an ocean of tulle to be kissed by handsome grooms (who've cleverly taken out the right mortgage with the right bank in advance). And even if the television cameras let us glimpse what happens after the walk down the aisle, children are cute, homes are House-and-Garden, and a gleaming new car pops up at the press of a button.

I've elaborated somewhat on this theme because the ability to differentiate between love and sex has become progressively harder to develop or maintain. Modern advertising adds up to powerful propaganda that persuades us — at the subconscious level — that media-type fairy-tales represent real-life criteria.

Thus if we know only too well we are not beautiful, sexy, rich or young, we feel we've been somehow robbed, and are undesirable as love or sex partners. Slowly this sense of deprivation chills into disappointment and finally hardens into bitterness. The vicious circle is complete. This situation is even more tragic and wasteful because the standards we could not possibly reach were false standards anyway, yet the undesirability of a bitter individual is very real indeed.

Nobody is totally immune from the impact of fairy-tale propaganda but the degree to which it gets through to individuals greatly depends on the particular personality patterns in any given chart.

Neptune — wherever the planet is in the chart and especially where hard aspects show up — provides fertile soil for illusions/fantasies to take root and flourish. If you find Neptune in the 5th house (which covers all forms of romantic hopes and dreams), the 'owner' of such a chart will find it harder to look at love realistically, hence can be more easily swept away on a wave of fantasies, and also become more likely to confuse sexual attraction with real love.

As we saw in Chapter 3, late twentieth-century living has wrought some staggering changes in the definition of marriage. Now, we can see that the same has happened with love and sex — which is why it's best to use the horoscope chart to look ahead and try to understand what you're getting into *before* you're in too deep!

Stated starkly in black and white, you're probably thinking this kind of approach to romance sounds far too cold-blooded. Really it isn't. All's fair in love and war as the proverb goes. And that's just another way of saying when you're tangling with Venus and/or Mars, you need all your wits about you.

Sun Signs in Love

Up to this point in the compatibility story, I've deliberately kept my comments about individual Sun signs to a minimum for a very important reason. They've been literally flogged to death in 'pop' astrology books, press features and by what I call 'bush astrologers'. ('Bush' used in that way is Australian slang for people who claim to have professional knowledge in some field but in fact know nothing at all!)

Sadly, since public interest in astrology began to escalate in the early 1970s, burbling about Sun signs has become a sort of party trick.

Certainly, some of the published material about them is reasonably accurate; some of it is nonsensical; all of it is far too generalized to offer reliable personality data.

Further, fixating on the Sun Sign alone has done the science of astrology great harm, by supplying ammunition to those who desire to denigrate it. Who hasn't heard someone sneering? 'I'm a Scorpio and so's my partner. We're nothing like each other. Astrology's a lot of rubbish!' And, in so-called compatibility analyses in magazines, where readers are blandly told they'll have a perfect marriage with Cancer partners but haven't a hope with Aries people. Misleading, over-generalized nonsense!

That's why I wish to stress throughout your investigations into compatibility that Sun signs must never be allowed to hog the limelight. On the other hand, that does not mean the role of the Sun sign in determining behaviour is insignificant. It always throws light on your true self, the core of your being, the basic 'You'.

Assuredly, its natural personality traits can be distorted, obscured or boosted by other chart indicators, but they can never be extinguished. So its influence cannot be ignored in assessing attraction and compatibility. Or, to mix a metaphor — when the chips are finally down in all relationships, the Sun sign always shines through.

So, now let's run through a set of fun exercises to prove the point. Read through the following list of twelve remarks typically made by each of the twelve Sun signs when planning 'to make a pass' at someone they've just met.

Note that I've used in each case the English translation of the name of each symbol — i.e. 'the Ram' instead of 'Aries', etc. — to help you visualize them more clearly. (Remember, the animal, mythological or human figure representing each sign was chosen to give an instant mental picture of its traits.)

After you've read and thought about each one, check through the précis of Sun sign data at the end and see why each one of the twelve thought and spoke as they did. This little exercise will also develop your ability to consider and blend the component qualities of each of the zodiacal signs.

If you feel you'd like more information than the short précis contains, please refer to *How to Astro-Analyse Yourself and Others*, Chapter 2.

Sun-sign switch-ons

Imagine you're at a party and dancing, one after the other, with twelve very attractive partners. Each represents a different one of the twelve Sun signs; each is also strongly attracted to you; each has sworn to state *exactly* what they're thinking and tell nothing but the truth!

The Ram	'Let's go some place right now and discover each other!'
The Bull	'I like your style. Present yourself for further inspection at my door — 8 o'clock sharp.'
The Twins	'Understand this is a "now" thing. I'm in the mood for you tonight but tomorrow I mightn't be!'
The Crab	'You've got to have heart. Lots and lots of heart! If not I won't play!'
The Lion	'Down on your knees at once! The Monarch is looking your way!'
The Virgin	'Sex is only an appetite, like eating and drinking. Let's keep our priorities in proper perspective from the outset!'
The Scales	'You might be the right one . . . on the present balance of probabilities but . . . there again . . . you mightn't!'
The Scorpion	'I *want* you! There's nothing more to be said!'
The Centaur	'The way I look at it, sex is more a sport. Does you a power of good too — provided you team up with the right partner!'
The Goat	'You've got to be "top-drawer" if you expect me to take you seriously. I plan to go a long way in life!'
The Water-Bearer	'Don't let's spoil this glorious dream by doing anything sordid — like getting into bed. We've got so much to talk about!'
The Fish	'Everybody's beautiful — in their own way. You are too! It's a beautiful world and love's the most beautiful thing of all!'

Now, you can see that each of the twelve Sun sign personalities looks at the opposite sex through very different eyes and seeks very different attributes in their chosen partners. Why? Let's check further with our précis:

Aries.   Averaged birthdate cycle: 21 March — 20 April.
Symbol: The Ram, the leader of the flock.
            Sign classification: Positive, Cardinal, Fire.
Implications: Will charge straight ahead at any threat or opportunity as does its symbol. Basic approach more extroverted, less studied (Positivity); goal pursuit more one-pointed, less broad-ranging (Cardinality); basic behaviour more impulsive, less prudent (Fire Element).

Taurus.   Averaged birthdate cycle: 21 April — 21 May.
Symbol: The Bull, the protector of the herd.
            Sign classification: Negative, Fixed, Earth.
Implications: Will stand back and calmly survey a situation before moving as does its symbol. Basic approach more introverted, less expressive (Negativity); goal pursuit more determined, less flexible (Fixity); basic behaviour more cautious, less spontaneous (Earth Element).

Gemini.   Averaged birthdate cycle: 22 May — 21 June.
Symbol: The Twins, the pair of fast-talking, high-flying brothers.
            Sign classification: Positive, Mutable, Air.
Implications: Will endlessly flit from one interest to the next as does its symbol. Basic approach more extroverted, less studied (Positivity); goal pursuit more adaptable, less consistent (Mutability); basic behaviour more communicative, less committed (Air Element).

Cancer.   Averaged birthdate cycle: 22 June — 23 July.
Symbol: The Crab, the sea-loving dweller of the caverns. Sign classification; Negative, Cardinal, Water.
Implications: Will keep out of sight and watch for chances as does its symbol. Basic approach more introverted, less expressive (Negativity); goal pursuit more one-pointed, less broad-ranging (Cardinality); basic behaviour more emotionaly based, less reasoning (Water Element).

Leo.   Averaged birthdate cycle: 24 July — 23 August.
Symbol: The Lion, the lordly king of the jungle.
            Sign classification: Positive, Fixed, Fire.

Implications: Will take a masterful, commanding stand, seeking homage as does its symbol. Basic approach more extroverted, less studied (Positivity); goal pursuit more determined, less flexible (Fixity); basic behaviour more impulsive, less prudent (Fire Element).

Virgo: Averaged birthdate cycle: 24 August — 23 September.
Symbol: The Virgin, the white-robed, untouched maiden.
            Sign classification: Negative, Mutable, Earth.
            Implications: Will take a perfectionist, stand-offish stand as
            does its symbol. Basic approach more introverted, less
            expressive (Negativity); goal pursuit more adaptable, less
            consistent (Mutability); basic behaviour more cautious,
            less spontaneous (Earth Element).

Libra.   Averaged birthdate cycle: 24 September — 23 October.
Symbol: The Scales, the perfectly poised, classically designed weigh-
            ing machine. Sign classification: Positive, Cardinal, Air.
Implications: Will take a balancing, weighing-up stand as does its symbol. Basic approach more extroverted, less studied (Positivity); goal pursuit more one-pointed, less broad-ranging (Cardinality); basic behaviour more communicative, less committed (Air element).

Scorpio.   Averaged birthdate cycle: 24 October — 22 November.
Symbol: The Scorpion, the long-stinged, solitary dweller of the
            rocks.
            Sign classification: Negative, Fixed, Water.
Implications: Will hide away, await an opportunity then leap out at the quarry as does its symbol. Basic approach more introverted, less expressive (Negativity); goal pursuit more determined, less flexible (Fixity); basic behaviour more emotionally based, less reasoning (Water element).

Sagittarius. Averaged birthdate cycle: 23 November — 22 December.
Symbol: The Centaur, the legendary bow-and-arrow-bearing
            creature that is half-human, half-horse.
            Sign classification: Positive, Mutable, Fire.
Implications: Will thunder in and out of adventures without pause as does its symbol. Basic approach more extroverted, less studied (Positivity); goal pursuit more adaptable, less consistent (Mutability); basic behaviour more impulsive, less prudent (Fire Element).

Capricorn.   Averaged birthdate cycle: 23 December — 20 January.
Symbol: The Mountain Goat, the high-climbing, sure-footed dweller of the peaks.
Sign classification: Negative, Cardinal, Earth.

Implications: Will assess the hazards of pursuit by testing the ground first as does its symbol. Basic approach more introverted, less expressive (Negativity); goal pursuit more one-pointed, less broad-ranging (Cardinality); basic behaviour more cautious, less spontaneous (Earth Element).

Aquarius.   Averaged birthdate cycle: 21 January — 19 February.
Symbol: The Water-Bearer, the handsome, always travelling seller of heavenly water.
Sign classification: Positive, Fixed, Air.

Implications: Will keep clear of anything that impedes freedom to move on as does its symbol. Basic approach more extroverted, less studied (Positivity); goal pursuit more determined, less flexible (Fixity); basic behaviour more communicative, less committed (Air Element).

Pisces.   Averaged birthdate cycle: 20 February — 20 March.
Symbol: The Fish, the bound-together, many-coloured dwellers of the deep.
Sign classification: Negative Mutable, Water.

Implication: Will look for peaceful, untroubled waters and swim whichever way the tide is flowing as does its symbol. Basic approach more introverted, less expressive (Negativity); goal pursuit more adaptable, less consistent (Mutability); basic behaviour more emotionally based, less reasoning (Water Element).

Special note for beginners

Take time off to note how the classifications of the twelve signs express their qualities differently according to the particular blend of them. To illustrate: Libra and Capricorn are both cardinal signs, thus visibly goal-oriented and somewhat pushy in achieving their aims *and* their own way. But Libra is a positive air sign and Capricorn is a negative earth sign. Thus the goal thrust is more easily and extrovertedly expressed in Libra and aims have a lighter, more intellectually slanted content, while Capricorn's goal thrust is less assured and more inhibited in outward expression and aims have a heavier, more solidly ambitious content.

To improve your skills, work through all the other signs in the above manner. You'll find it makes successful synthesis of conflicting traits in final analyses much easier to attain.

Signs on the Fifth: Expectations of Love and Children

The 5th house itself is not an angular house so its effects on the overall life pattern of each individual is considerably less dramatic. Therefore there is no need to discuss the effect of the sign on its cusp in the detail we did in preceding chapters on the 4th and 7th, both of which *are* angular houses.

Nevertheless, the sign on the 5th will frequently attract individuals born under it or of the element it represents. Further, it noticeably colours your attitude to whatever children come under your personal control — not only your own offspring but those of partners, for example.

This last is well worth watching carefully if you plan to take on step-children (an ever more common situation today). Coping with them successfully is never exactly a bowl of cherries at the best of times and if the sign on your 5th clashes strongly with the signs on their own parent's, step as carefully as if you were walking on eggs. Mishandling of your lover's children — in or out of marriage — is tantamount to planting the kiss of death on the entire relationship. Parental attitudes spring from the depths of the psyche (as we've seen earlier) so cannot be attacked with impunity — even by the love partner.

I well recall an example of this danger. Subject was a strongly Cancer-type female, also with Cancer on her 5th house cusp. She was on her third marriage, this time to a Sagittarian male, whose 15-year-old son was also born under the sign of the Centaur. (Remember, signs often do repeat through families.)

The boy's mother had died after a long illness only a year before. He was angry, resentful at having a successor quickly thrust upon him and ready to trample anyone who came too close. His Cancer step-mother appeared to be totally oblivious to his quite undisguised dislike. At a dinner party, I watched her cuddle and cling to him (as the sign dictates) but with one eye on her new husband, his father, in an obvious effort to impress.

I did not know the father's chart patterns but his whole attitude to children was clearly the antithesis of hers. The boy seethed, the father clenched his teeth, but still she went on with the mothering display. The end result was the boy left home the day after he left school and never returned. The marriage itself survived miserably and only because a new baby arrived to tighten the knot.

A cautionary tale! And one to be remembered even in cases where children do belong to the existing marriage partners. Clashing ideas on child-rearing have broken or damaged more marriages than bear thinking about.

So, when in doubt about matters concerning offspring, look at the parent's two charts and especially the attributes of the sign on the 5th house cusp in each case.

While we're on the general subject of children — 'the fruits of love' as they were once described, which explains why they belong to the 5th house — we'll take a closer look at whether you're likely to find yourself in the role of Mother or Father.

Parenthood: To Be or Not to Be? Indicators of Fertility

Once upon a time — long ago in the days before science moved in on the baby business — pregnancy was either a matter for wild rejoicing or desperate tooth-gnashing. There was virtually nothing much anyone could do about it. Children arrived. Or they didn't. They were wanted. Or they weren't. And that was definitely that!

Today, if a female is rather more fertile than she fancies, medical science has a variety of answers. If the reverse applies and the longed-for infant doesn't appear, medical science can come up with quite a few ways of fixing that problem too. But what science *cannot* change is the female psyche. That has remained pretty much the same since Homo Sapiens first emerged on Planet Earth, and in double-quick time (evolution-wise) made himself *the* dominant species.

There have *always* been women who wanted offspring and women who did not. The only real difference is — for the last couple of decades in particular — females have been more willing to state their feelings with regard to motherhood. And males have been rather more willing to listen.

Nevertheless, what we *say* on a topic of vital concern to us — and producing a child is certainly in that category — is not necessarily what we *feel* in our guts. A woman may say in all honesty that she would dearly love to become a mother yet subconsciously fear her competence in that role and hence create a subconscious block against pregnancy.

But the horoscope chart will always reveal the truth in this as in all life sectors, so let's look at what indicators promise fertility or lack of it.

Since time immemorial, the signs of the Zodiac have been divided into classifications under the somewhat old-fashioned title of 'Fruitfulness'. Dr H. L. Cornell, Honorary Professor of Medical Astrology at the First National University of Naturopathy and Allied Sciences, Newark, USA, devotes almost two pages of small type to the subject in his weighty 958-page *Encyclopaedia of Medical Astrology*. Readers interested in determining their fertility can gain valuable information from the doctor's research; but, a small word of warning to beginners in astrological studies: you need to be fully conversant with the science before dipping into the encyclopaedia. To cram in the vast wealth of knowledge available, Dr Cornell uses abbreviations and technical terminology that aren't easy for novices to comprehend.

It is also vital to remember that determining fertility is not just a matter of checking on your own Sun sign and your partner's. These will certainly give some clues as to your basic reactions to the thought of or existence of children. But the Sun sign is only the tip of the proverbial iceberg.

Here follows a brief summary of a few of Dr Cornell's pointers and my own research has turned up the same answers.

Fruitful Signs
Most fruitful: Cancer, Scorpio and Pisces.
Rather fruitful: Taurus, Libra and Sagittarius.
Less fruitful: Aries, Capricorn and Aquarius.
Least fruitful: Gemini, Virgo and Leo.

Planetary Indicators of Fertility
Moon, Venus and Jupiter are what Dr Cornell describes as the 'Givers of Children'. Helpful influences from these planets affecting the 5th and 11th houses of the horoscope chart promise offspring if desired. Greater certainty of parenthood is indicated if both partners show patterns that add up to fertility in their charts. Aspects to planets in the 5th and 11th houses must also be considered and also whether the signs on the cusp of these houses fall into a fruitful category.

However, it must be solidly stressed that the foregoing pointers cannot be taken as representing the complete picture. For example, an empty 5th house with a less fruitful sign on its cusp does not imply you'll be childless. What an empty 5th means, in my view, is simply that you will never need to express yourself and your creativity through your offspring.

Tough planets in child-oriented houses do not necessarily deny children either. Uranus or Pluto in the 5th are quite capable of producing offspring who grow up to be more of a handful than a barrel of monkeys.

Another interesting pointer that Dr. Cornell emphasizes is that there need to be comparable degrees of fertility in both potential parents. This is why if individuals change partners, they may discover they can suddenly have children or just as suddenly cannot.

Of course, as a psychologist, I have noted in discussions with clients of child-bearing age that even if a chart promises unlimited fertility, you must look to see if repressions or some other form of subconscious blocking are preventing it.

Then, you have to explore farther afield into the early home experiences of the individual, how they were conditioned to view marriage and parenthood, etc., often right around the chart.

One last point that most people have probably never given a thought to. Man's the *only* animal on this planet who is able to engage in sexual intercourse at any time and purely for pleasure instead of for the purpose of reproduction. Humanity is designed like that. So, don't think if you're not into the Romper Room scene, you're flying in the face of Nature.

Fifth House Planets: Their Effect on Love Affairs and Children

The more important planetary pointers with regard to children, their existence and behaviour towards them, have already been covered in the preceding parenthood section. With regard to love affairs, similar rules to those discussed in the marriage chapter apply.

Empty 5th houses do not deny opportunity for or success in romantic liaisons, but the personality's greatest drives are not directed solely towards them. On the other hand, a group of 5th house planets (a stellium) will stress — sometimes excessively — the desire to develop through love experiences or the rearing of children or both.

Also (as we saw before with the marriage house planets), the presence of planets in the 5th whose energies do not combine comfortably, such as freedom-mad Uranus and dogmatically dutiful Saturn, is creative of ambivalent behaviour, swings from one extreme to the other, odd inconsistencies which not only puzzle their 'owner' but also those involved with him/her.

Yet another valuable clue to love behaviour is to be found in the 5th house and derives from the 5th's role as the precursor of marriage. It fills in the background scenery — like a theatrical stage full of props — at the time the decision to wed was taken.

Hence, to a limited extent, the 5th pictures the earliest period of marriage. Those heady nights and days when romantic dreams are still floating like champagne bubbles round the double bed.

In this manner, the 5th provides a vivid contrast with the 7th, the marriage house itself — that house which shows the state of the union when it has settled into its permanent pattern.

From this view, we can see crystallized in charts the hard facts of living day-in day-out with another human being. Romance is for fun but marriage means business!

Lastly, as you work your way through the 5th house planets, you'll note their meanings are somewhat similar to those for the 7th house. This is because, in both 5th ad 7th affairs, the emphasis is on one form or other of liaisons — brief and romantically triggered as liaisons can be when looking at the 5th; always longer in term and less responsive to illusion when looking at the 7th.

Fifth House Data at a Glance

The focus on the 5th	Reveals all types of romantic interests and love affairs throughout adult life; type of individuals who present themselves in role of lovers; kind of pleasures enjoyed alone or with love partners; attitude towards children; overall creativity.
The planets in the 5th	Give further indications as to above; help or hinder love affairs and handling of children; introduce ease or stress in this life sector.
The aspects to the 5th	Link up other houses with love affairs/children;

easy aspects promise assistance from other life activities; awkward aspects threaten other conflicting outside interests.

Sun in 5th: Infers *self-esteem* dependent on romantic satisfaction. Added sensuality possible. Desire to gain acclaim for own creativity which may be channelled either through children or through artistic achievements. May strive to rule those cared about. Expects admiration and gratification of desires.

Sun here indicates the self strives to attract others by displays of power.

Moon in 5th: Infers *emotional outlet* required from differing love experiences. Fluctuating responses possible. May try to relieve inner tensions through creative pursuits. Easily becomes stressed through disputes with lovers or children. Expects acceptance of changeable moods. Generally very responsive.

Moon here indicates the self strives to attract others by displays of emotion.

Mercury in 5th: Infers *intellectual needs* determine type and variety of love experience. May place intelligence before all other qualities in partners. Usually expects cleverness in children as well. More communicative type, with a talent that can be applied creatively. Several love affairs possible.

Mercury here indicates the self strives to attract others by displays of intellectual skills.

Venus in 5th: Infers *love expectations* seek pleasure and romance through partners. Good looks and visible charm rated above other qualities. Requires lovers to be equally interested in fast-moving, fun relationships. Usually has physically attractive children. May prefer to view surface glamour instead of realities. Usually tries for harmony.

Venus here indicates the self strives to attract others by displays of personal charm.

Mars in 5th: Infers *sexual drives* less controlled and tend to force pursuit of fast satisfaction through various love affairs. Energies also attract to dangerous or highly competitive sports and sometimes gambling too. Sexual vitality rated first in choice of partners. May take up a belligerent attitude with children. Over-indulgence of own passions and overstrain to the body possible.

Mars here indicates the self strives to attract others by displays of physical desirability.

Jupiter in 5th: Infers *sense of optimism* surrounds relationships with lovers/children. Wealth and rank rated above other qualities. Usually makes good first social impression on others. Seeks continuing pleasure in romantic situations and likes love scenes to be enacted against luxurious backgrounds. Children often talented in skills that bring financial benefits.

Jupiter here indicates the self strives to attract others by displays of influence.

Saturn in 5th: Infers *self-control* takes priority in responding to romantic advances or child-rearing. Possible awkward social posture may disconcert others and restrict pleasures. Reliability/common sense rated highly in partners. May feel guilty about enjoying the self. Over-caution and disciplinary actions likely if lovers/children transgress. Some creative skills present but may be blocked.

Saturn here indicates the self strives to attract others by displays of strength.

Uranus in 5th: Infers *desire for personal space* fears ties with lovers or responsibility for children. May switch from affair to affair to avoid permanency. Usually very unconventional about relationships — in both type and partner chosen. May exhibit sudden spurts of creativity. Sometimes produces off-beat children and breaks links with them. Possible over-stress on personal independence.

Uranus here indicates the self strives to attract others by displays of unorthodoxy.

Neptune in 5th: Infers desire for *spiritual development* seeks direction and inspiration through lovers and children. May be regularly imposed upon or tricked by either. Romantic daydreaming and regular fantasizing possible. Often easily seduced — mentally or bodily. Usually very creative but may lack application. Children likely to drift out of contact.

Neptune here indicates the self strives to attract others by displays of vulnerability.

Pluto in 5th: Infers *subconscious drives* compel toward self-discovery through all types of love experiences. Obsessive behaviour possible. Intensity and domination likely towards romantic attachments and children. Usually finds it hard to control possessiveness. Alienation of affections may result from over-demand. Marked need for creative outlet. Power-seeking in relationships can constitute a danger.

Pluto here indicates the self strives to attract others by displays of insight.

Aspects to the Fifth:
Further Clues to Romantic Attachments

As we have previously discussed the effect of the major planetary aspects in previous chapters, we won't go over the same ground again in this section. Remember, the interpretation of any significant aspect between any two or more planets does not vary *in essence* irrespective of which houses and which planets the aspects link together. For example: Sun square Moon has the same basic effect on the manner in which the personality looks at itself whether such an aspect links, say, the 1st and the 10th houses or the 9th and the 12th houses.

The principle to work on is that any major aspect will help or hinder the affairs of the houses it links but must express according to the attributes of the signs in which it appears. To illustrate briefly: Let's say the Sun in Pisces in the 5th house is in square to the Moon in Gemini in the 8th house. Any square aspect between Sun (will) and Moon (emotions) creates extreme inner tension, thrusting towards contradictory behaviour as the self must struggle desperately to satisfy two vastly differing needs. But in our example, that square aspect will have to express its energy according to the traits of Pisces and Gemini — both mutable signs, implying endless bending this way and that. A battle between emotion and reason.

Finally, the square has to seek outlets through activities, which create conflict of interests between 5th and 8th house affairs. Thus it can generate squabbles and confused reactions from the following type of situation.

The individual with the square aspect and the love partner decide they wish to buy property in joint names with inherited moneys, thus bringing together the 5th (lovers) and the 8th (money of others). Trouble will almost certainly follow unless great care and expert legal advice is taken, due to the fact that the individual with the square aspect behaves in a confusing, changeable manner.

The above example will serve as a basic yardstick for interpretation of aspects in all compatibility analyses as it reminds you to:

● Look at each aspect and its meaning.
● Check the signs it links and their traits.
● Consider the two life sectors (houses) it is linking together.

Naturally, as we're keeping the spotlight trained on the 5th house in this chapter, we would interpret all aspects affecting it from the 5th house standpoint, i.e. their influence over love, romantic attachments and children.

There is, however, one further aspect that's worth considering at this stage. I haven't singled it out before because it is not a major one. Still, it can give unexpected trouble on occasions. Its name is the 'semi-sextile'. When you note, while cross-referencing two charts, that Partner A has planets in semi-sextile to Partner B's, read on with care!

Propinquity Blues

As you first start out upon the long hard road which leads to successful and accurate analysis of compatibility between two individuals, the semi-sextile looks like a mild-mannered, unpretentious aspect that wouldn't rock anybody's boat.

Indeed, many textbooks describe it as 'mildly beneficial' or more formally as 'a 30 degree aspect'. But beware! Take care! Despite the fact that it can only occur between adjacent signs, e.g. Virgo/Libra, Cancer/Leo, recent research proves semi-sextiles are nothing like as innocuous as they look. Some researchers point out each sign picks up the karma of its predecessor in the zodiac and thus is not all that favourably disposed towards said predecessor.

Others suggest the semi-sextile can add up to a genuine nail-biter in compatibility analyses. And when you think about it, you'll have to agree. After all, how *can* lordly, dramatic, 'tell-me-you-adore-me' Leo handle the cut-and-dried pragmatism of his zodiac neighbour Virgo? Or how does jovial, 'she'll-be-right' Sagittarius cope with intense, do-or-die Scorpio, described by that rare creature — a humorous astrological author — as 'an Olympic sulker'?

I have also noted in hundreds of cases where compatibility in love is the major issue that even the two Mercurys of the prospective partners will often effectively block easy communication when the aspect is a semi-sextile. There is little or no common mental meeting ground. One partner might just as well have been talking French and the other Greek!

Or — to transfer our test scene from the boardroom to the boudoir — what price an airy, flighty Venus in Gemini deftly dealing with a sentimental, clinging Venus in Cancer?

All of which goes to show that propinquity in the zodiac can sometimes cause us to wind up singing the blues — just as quickly as the more challenging aspects.

Finally, before we travel on to farther fields, let's drop in once more on our specimen couple — Harry and Helen — to inspect their situation from the doorway of the 5th house.

Fifth house cusp

Harry has a water sign there; Helen has a fire sign. Problems again with this pair. Harry, an air type, becomes uncharacteristically emotional, even vulnerable where romance and children are concerned. He handles both somewhat tentatively. Helen doesn't buy this approach at all. Although she is an earth type, she's ready for fireworks in this life sector. Significantly, when they met, she made the first advance.

Planets in the 5th

Harry's 5th house has Jupiter and Uranus ensconced therein. So, despite the fact that air types are rarely child-oriented or secretly romantic, he *is*! Helen's 5th house is bare as a bone. Being an earth type and hence dutiful, she won't deny him children, but they're certainly not her favourite forte. She's inclined to handle them *and* him forcefully. He backs off rather shaken. Meanwhile, Harry's Jupiter has duly delivered two talented, attractive offspring which fact pleases him no end. So all goes fairly well there, until both children are old enough for Uranus to turn them into wayward, off-beat types who break filial ties without a qualm. Harry can't understand what went wrong. He blames Helen's style of mothering.

It is interesting to note that three years after they were married, Harry suddenly announced (in a fit of pique) that he was already a father when he met Helen. At the age of 20, while living overseas, a stormy short-lived affair had produced an unexpected, undesired child. He gave the girl a sum of money and broke contact completely. Uranus on the job again! This scenario is not uncommon with the Great Disruptor in the 5th.

Aspects to the 5th

As Helen has no planets there, there are no aspects to further affect her attitude. Harry has a set of two, both fairly helpful, linking to the 3rd (communication, educational skills) and the 1st (self-expression). These imply he can siphon off some of his 5th house disappointments by applying his brains and spreading his intellectual interests for one thing. For another, the talented, attractive children — although they weren't up to scratch as far as his emotional expectations of fatherhood went — have certainly done no damage to his self-image. He supposes it was all more or less worth it!

Sorry to say, the 5th house scene didn't offer much in the way of amelioration of the clash-points between Harry and Helen we saw in earlier comparisons. But since neither could be described as sentimental, both took the view that this was the way the marital cookie crumbled. Nobody wept for long.

Now, as before, in your own charts, blend in the new personality data we've collected from the 5th house and decide whether it's taken you further along the path to successful union or set you back a step or two.

Love — Forties Style and Eighties Style

Since this has been a chapter devoted to romance, I feel it's appropriate to round it off with two real-life love stories. The first was told to me by a middle-aged client some years ago and, unfortunately, I have now forgotten the details of her chart and her husband's. All I remember is that she was born under Virgo and he under Taurus. Not only does it show the two signs in action but also offers a nostalgic contrast between how young people felt in the 1940's compared with how too many of them feel today.

Scene: the open bushland that once surrounded Sydney. Characters: one 17-year-old Virgo girl and one 18-year-old Taurus boy. Year: 1944.

The Virgo, appropriately gowned in a white, summer dress with long fair hair, flowing down her back, was gathering wild mushrooms in a paddock. The young Bull male was peacefully browsing by a riverbank. After a few minutes, the Virgo climbed up on a fence to drink in the earth scents of summer. (Earth scenes always turn earth people on!) The young Bull male looked up, spotted the golden hair, and — although he'd never seen the girl before in his life — thundered off in pursuit. Across the paddock, under the fence, and scooping her up to his massive shoulders, ran off with her, shouting: 'I won't put you down till you give me a kiss!'

She gave him a kiss. And (sounds like a fairy story these days, doesn't it?) a couple of years later they were married and they lived happily ever after.

I thought sadly of this little tale not long ago when I attended a Sunday lecture at Sydney University. Above the handbasins in the washroom, a girl student of the Aquarian Age 1980s had written the following verse:

> Read up your books,
> Push through your papers,
> Pick up your medals,
> Sleep with your strangers . . .
> It all seems kind of empty, doesn't it!

Maybe in the next few decades we'll all gradually adjust to the new age and the Brave New World it brings. But it won't be easy even for those as young as the author of that doleful little verse. The romance of the Piscean Age — despite the fact that much of it *was* based on fantasy — still remains a very human dream.

Journey's End in Pluto Meetings

Inscrutable, extremist Pluto is scarcely a planet you regularly associate with lovers' reunions and happy endings. Yet he *does* have his softer side as I discovered when I checked up the planetary background to the following set of quite remarkable events.

The story begins long ago in the early years of World War II. A young soldier (whom we'll call Ted) met a young army nurse (whom we'll call June). For him, she was 'the only girl in the whole world'. For her, he was 'a nice young fellow' but she didn't want to tie herself down before she'd had what used to be described as 'her fling'.

He was sent overseas. He wrote her mountains of letters. She replied. But then along came someone else — a smooth-talking, girl-chasing sailor. June couldn't resist him. In next to no time, they were married. Within a year, she had a baby son but by the end of the war she discovered that was *all* she had. The sailor was gone. Not down with his ship but off with another girl. June reared her son alone, finally obtained a divorce and decided she'd write men off for good.

Nearly thirty years passed. Then one day, June took a new job in a new suburb, and thought she'd spend her lunch-hour wandering round the shopping centre. 'I don't know why to this day,' she told me, 'but as I passed by a tailor's shop something *made* me look in. At the very same minute, the tailor looked out into the street and our eyes met. I'm not sure which of us shouted the loudest. I was screaming 'Teddy' and he was yelling 'Junie'. The next minute he was throwing his arms around me and I was laughing and crying all at once. Just as if we'd only said goodbye yesterday instead of way back in 1941.

'I suppose we must have looked ridiculous. Two middle-aged people acting like kids. But I'd thought of Teddy many times in the intervening years and realized what a fool I'd been. I never dreamt Fate would give me a second chance like that. But it did. Teddy was a widower and I was divorced so we got married a month later. And it's been wonderful. Just wonderful!'

This entire story is true. I've changed only the names and some of the details to prevent identification. But what, astrologically speaking, triggered the final event pattern?

June had Neptune in a hard aspect which frequently causes the tendency to pursue romance with a capital 'R' and promotes fairy-tale type illusions as to the nature of love. This, among other chart factors, set the scene for the unwise, impractical marriage to the sailor and the heartaches which inevitably followed it. But Pluto, too, was strongly positioned in June's chart and with the aid of Saturn, he eventually repaired the damage.

To explain this last requires a brief comment on Future Life Trend forecasting (which will be the subject of my next book), as it involves interpretation of planetary transits.

In June's case, Saturn was approaching the end of his 29½ year cycle, so he obviously had a hand in the proceedings. He had forced June to learn her lessons in all those years so that Pluto could take over when the time was right. At the time June looked into the tailor's shop, Pluto was in an exact trine to Venus as he transited June's 7th house. This aspect is one that often does bring back people from the past, offering the chance to regenerate an old love relationship.

Added to this fact, Pluto's aspects cover considerable periods of time because of the planet's very slow motion. Thus as Pluto came into orb with Venus, the events were gradually put in train and the stage was set — to do what Pluto invariably achieves: a total transformation of the life.

'Journeys end in lovers' meetings,' as Shakespeare said. For June and her Teddy, the journey was a long one but they both had the courage to make sure it had a happy ending.

Quick reference check-points
Plus or Minus indicators of Romantic Expectations

The Lion's share of love: The sign of Leo is the natural ruler of the 5th house, so in all romantic attachments, there's a shadow of lion-like behaviour, despite what other influences affect a given chart. So to focus the picture clearly, let's listen to actual comments I've collected, made to their lovers by Leo types — remembering that Lion personalities do not take kindly to any pussy-footing around with their affections. For example:

> Lady Lion to Centaur Male (per overseas telephone); 'I've decided to marry you.'
> Centaur Male, breathing hard: 'Can I call you back on that?'

> Lady Lion to Fish Male (again per telephone): 'I think it's about time we got married.'
> Fish Male (swiftly): 'What an interesting idea! Did I tell you I've just sold a painting?'

> Lady Lion to Goat Male (in person): 'If you want to go to bed with me, you'll have to marry me right away.'
> Goat Male (after brief period of silent reflection): 'Do you want a formal wedding?'

History v. Romance: Psychoanalysts researching the history of love and marriage in Western society point out that romantic attraction as the *sole* basis for marriage is a purely twentieth-century 'invention'. Up till then (stories and fables aside), couples were married off by parental arrangement to consolidate land holdings, to cement family connections, for solidly practical reasons far removed from romance. While this practice continued, 'old maids' were virtually unknown. Women had obvious value as home-makers, workers, child-bearers. None of these roles required beauty, glamour or even physical attractiveness, which meant that nobody landed 'on the self'. Compatibility as to upbringing and background was assured. Further, many researchers maintain this system worked, and a whole lot better as a rule than ours does. So digest these observations slowly if your own charts show over-emphasis on romanticism. It plainly is *not* the best foundation for lasting unions.

Killer talk . . . killer gestures: American therapist Dr I. Kassorla in her book on love and family problems, *Putting It All Together* applies the above highly descriptive terms to people who unwittingly destroy relationships by the negative way they talk and behave towards those cared about. If your own charts show evidence of negativity in signs, planets or aspects, keep a sharp lookout for the presence of recurring. 'Killer Talk' or 'Killer Gestures'. Here are a few leads from Dr Kassorla's lengthy list. Note that negatives — like don't, can't, shouldn't — dominate 'killer talk', e.g. 'What? You *didn't* pick up the dry-cleaning?' . . . 'I *can't* stand the way you act at parties!', etc.

'Killer gestures' are a dangerous bunch too. Among them are — pointing the finger, refusing to reply, rolling the eyes towards heaven, raising the eyebrows and sighing gustily.

As you can see, every example of this type of speech or behaviour is custom-built to discomfort, hurt and alienate anyone at whom it is directed. Throw in a good dash of sarcasm such as 'Eating with you is as good as a visit to the zoo!' and it's curtains for the relationship.

Love in the late afternoon: Possibly one of the greatest fears experienced by men and women over 40 is the thought that the loss of youthful attractiveness means the end of love and sex life. Not so! Agreed, in the last couple of decades the unspoken statements that 'Young = beautiful', 'Old = ugly' have dominated reactions to a dangerous degree and to the point that too many people have begun to believe they're already losing their appeal even by the time they're 25.

As we saw earlier in this chapter, this false view emanates from current obsessions with qualities that are purely and narrowly physical. So don't let it get to you if you *are* in the older age groupings.

Some charts push heavily towards later life unions: remember the Sun position, Saturn for example. So, again, don't be hustled and hassled into tying yourself to whoever happens to be handy when it is far better to wait calmly. Take care also to avoid being influenced by individuals who say sexual activity and displays of physical love are improper in older couples. That idea is psychologically and biologically ridiculous. Those who push it are invariably frustrated and embittered themselves.

Cementing the union: I often think of a psychology lecturer during my university days, who used to say to us: 'Some people like children in the abstract but *not* in the concrete.' An apt statement and well worth reflecting upon before you enter on a permanent relationship. The thought of pretty little feet, pitter-pattering about the house is very different from the reality. Thus if you deeply desire children and your partner does not want them — the chart will show the true situation no matter what is actually said on the subject — think long and hard before any knot is tied. This is a problem fraught with anguish.

Moreover, many women (and occasionally men too) have children for the express purpose of using them to cement a relationship. A strongly child-oriented sign such as Cancer tends to think along these lines. Again, it is a dangerous view. Bad for the children. Bad for the parents.

When personal planets point away: It's not uncommon to find charts where those planets which specifically influence love and marriage attitudes — i.e. Moon, Venus and Mars are all located in houses which do not relate to those life areas. The effect of this type of placement is to direct the planetary energies away from personal concerns to other objectives. To illustrate: the effect of Mars in the 5th, say, is quite different in a love/sex context to Mars in the 2nd. As we observed, Mars in the 5th is ready to leap head-first into romantic adventures. Mars in the 2nd is busy boosting attractiveness by stacking up money to prove it. Keep an eye on this pointer.

And so, we come to the end of our inspection of the 5th house and all it presages. We've covered a lot of ground and looked at it from many angles because your compatibility in love and sex are of supreme import when picking your partner.

There's only one more chart area to be examined before we prepare sample compatibility analyses and fill in our Compatibility Rating Tables. This last, but far from least, consideration fills the next chapter where we learn how to look beneath the social mask of yourself and your partner — the mask that's painted and put together by the Ascendant and Mercury.

CHAPTER FIVE

Behind the Social Mask: Ascendant and Mercury — Their Role in Mutual Attraction

First Appearances

'Speak that I might know thee' . . . 'He who smiles and smiles and smiles and is a villain'. As ever, Shakespeare had the words for it and in these two quotations he neatly summed up two vital factors in personality presentation. The spoken word — what is said and how it's said: the surface manner, which may or may not conceal a totally different self beneath.

Speech, spoken or written, plus all forms of communication between individuals, belong to the domain of Mercury. The planet dictates not only how we think but *how we want others to hear* us.

The surface manner (or projected personality) is a kind of overlay, masking to a greater or lesser extent the true personality. This is the province of the Ascendant (or rising sign) which dictates *how we want others to see us*. Both are of supreme importance, psychologically and astrologically, as they create the first, and hence vital, impression we make on others.

On that enchanted evening when you see the stranger across the crowded room, you're drawn towards him/her primarily because of the initial physical impression you gain — type of looks, build, style of dress, facial expression, body language. All these add up to a powerful signal which alerts your senses like a fire alarm. You like what you see and you want to see more of it.

Each one of the above mix of physical characteristics is largely determined by your stranger's Ascendant. When you find yourself instantly attracted to someone, the Ascending Sign of that person stimulates responsive signs and aspects in your own chart. Automatically you edge your way closer so that you can hear your stranger speak. The sound of the voice, its tone, what is being said, either enhances the sudden attraction or drops it twitching in its tracks.

Again, the Ascendant plays a role here but the basic manner of communication is much more a matter for Mercury. If your stranger's Mercury sign also strikes a chord in your own chart, you're as good as hooked. If not, you may walk back across the crowded room as fast as you decently can.

Thus the significance of first impressions in finding *and* keeping your perfect partner must never be underestimated. Especially today, when Aquarian Age social behaviour, with its emphasis on casual contact between the sexes, can determine the fate of a possible relationship on a five-minute once-over!

As we saw in Chapters 3 and 4, the last couple of decades have revolutionized the meaning of marriage/commitment, love and romance. Now, we must face the fact that the ways in which boy meets girl have been whirled off in new directions too. What a far cry it is from the family-planned, family-supervised pairings of the past to the 'Hey, you! Want to dance?', swiftly followed by 'My place or yours?' routines of the present.

Clearly then (and perhaps sadly), this is the first time in human history where potential partners are sized up, checked out, accepted or discarded after little more than a glance plus a few words — well-chosen or otherwise.

Few wait long enough to see if beneath that plain exterior beats the proverbial heart of gold. Many discover later to their cost that beneath that sexy exterior beats a heart of stone.

In earlier times, the first-impressions factor was far less dangerously prominent. Social groups were more closely knit, partner-seekers usually knew each other fairly well *before* an advance was made and so character traits other than those immediately visible and audible had time to show themselves. Agreed, this set-up did not guarantee perfect relationships but at least it did minimize the mistake of buying a book by its cover. Still, no one can turn back the clock so we have to take late twentieth-century living as we find it. And *that* means looking long and hard at personality factors created and put on show by the Ascendant and Mercury.

Since ours is an age when communication is top of the list, we'll tackle Mercury first and begin by examining the planet through its ancient symbol — the fleet-footed messenger of the gods.

Back in Chapter 2, we observed how all the planets were named after the deity which most resembled their influence on human behaviour. As mentioned earlier, visualizing each astrological symbol, signs or planets, is the fastest, most effective method of understanding their interpretations. Every school-teacher knows pupils catch on most quickly through visual learning programmes: every newspaper owner knows the huge hole that the *visual* medium of television has made in his profits. Hence it never ceases to astound me that so many astrology textbook authors fail to point out the instant *and* lasting insight gained from visualizing the symbol of the sign or planet they are describing. Indeed, some writers without qualifications in psychology do not even appear to be aware of its existence!

You'll see more precisely what I'm getting at with symbolism if you spare a second now to visualize the god Mercury. In classical mythology, he is always shown forever rushing here, there and everywhere on his winged sandals. Spreading news, passing on messages, stirring the gossip pot, keeping his ear to the right keyholes. A restless, volatile, talkative, on-the-go character, who is able to put himself across glibly, easily, convincingly.

Think of the planet Mercury in that way and you'll immediately appreciate why anyone ruled by him or who has the planet well placed and well aspected in the natal chart, cannot help but act in a mercurial manner. They *are* glib, easy, convincing talkers and thus usually make an attractive first impression.

Conversely, those with Mercury badly placed and/or poorly aspected have the reverse effect on others, especially at first acquaintance. They may sound awkward, cold, halting, even embarrassingly uncommunicative. The question 'What do you say after you say Hallo?' seems to hang agonizingly before their eyes. The silences feel like they'll go on all night.

Yet, the smoothest talkers are very often the smoothest operators too — which doesn't make them the best of bets in long-term relationships — so don't discount the merits of potential partners who haven't the god-given way with words. Drawing them out may be as heavy going as cycling uphill but the end result is often worth the effort required to break through the communication barrier.

To decide if you and yours are easy or awkward communicators and how your mentalities match up, we check Mercury's sign position first — in the same manner as we did with the other four personal planets in Chapter 1.

Mind and Ego — How Do They Mix?

Due to the astronomical fact that Mercury is the closest planet to the Sun in the solar system, it always occupies the same zodiacal sign as the Sun *or* those immediately adjacent to that sign. So let's see where that takes us.

In cases where both the Sun and Mercury are, say, in Leo, the ego (Sun) and mentality (Mercury) will reinforce each other in the exhibition of strongly Lion personality traits. This type would not only behave Lion-style, he/she would also think Lion-style.

However, where you find the Sun, say in Aries and Mercury in Taurus, a contrary pull in personality appears. This type behaves Ram-style and thinks Bull-style. The fiery competitive dash is blocked by slower, more ponderous deliberating.

Tuning into your partner's private wave-length on the mental level is vital since consistent sharing of ideas and interests lays the best foundation for continuing compatibility.

So, let's whip through a short list of famous names to get the feel of the Sun/Mercury mix in action.

Napoleon. Emperor and conqueror. Born 15 Augst 1769; Sun in Leo; Mercury in Leo. No conflict here. He saw himself as the king of all he surveyed and thought like that too. His Lion-style ability to organize and order around thousands of Frenchmen while still retaining their love and admiration wrote the story of his success.

Kepler. Astrologer and astronomer. Born 27 December 1571. Sun in Capricorn; Mercury in Capricorn. Cohesion here. With both mind and will working tirelessly together, he formulated theories on planetary orbits which revolutionized astronomy and astrology and prepared the ground for his great seventeenth-century successor, Sir Isaac Newton, born 25 December 1642. A fellow Capricorn, Newton's birthdate was only two days before Kepler's, although he was not born until some twelve years after Kepler had died. Doubtless, the shared Sun sign would have allowed Newton to see into Kepler's thinking as clearly as if they had talked to each other. Interesting to note too that both these intellectual giants continued to practise as astrologers despite the jibes of lesser minds.

Shakespeare. Playwright and poet. Born 23 April 1564. Sun in Taurus;

Mercury in Aries. Some contradictions here. The Bull ego saw where the royal coffers lay and set out purposefully to open them. The Ram mentality assured the prodigious output necessary to win fame plus the fast, incisive thinking which creates narrative energy.

Shaw. Playwright and author. Born 26 July 1856. Sun in Leo; Mercury in Cancer. Contradictions again. The lordly self-assurance and organized creative drive of the Lion set his sights on the stage while the Crab mind mixed in excellent memory and tenacity in applying intellectual skills.

Bob Hope. Comedian and actor. Born 29 May 1903. Sun in Gemini; Mercury in Gemini. Cohesion here. The wise-cracking, verbal acrobatics of the Twins somersaulted him into the words business, kept him alert to public tastes *and* in the limelight long after his contemporaries had died or dropped from sight.

The Mind Behind the Face:
Mercury Signs and Basic Mental Attitude

Mercury in Aries. Symbolized by the Ram, Aries is a positive, cardinal, fire sign. Thus, manner of thinking, speaking and writing aims for a fast, thrusting, battering effect. Intent is to burn up opposition, to show the self as an intellectual leader. To some the incisive cut and thrust is mentally stimulating, arousing. To others, it is wounding, reckless, inflaming.
   Behavioural keyword for Aries: 'I am'. Thus Aries talk runs on the '*I* think . . .*I* say . . . *I* expect' track.

Mercury in Taurus. Symbolized by the Bull, Taurus is a negative, fixed, earth sign. Thus, manner of thinking, speaking and writing aims for solid, slow, well-mulled-over expression of ideas. Intent is to bulldoze opposition, to show the self as a stable protector of tried and true standards. To some the unhurried, browsing through thoughts is mentally calming. To others, it is boring, repetitive, stick-in-the-mud.
   Behavioural keyword for Taurus: 'I have'. Thus Taurus talk runs on the 'Look at all the good solid ideas I've stacked up for you' track.

Mercury in Gemini. Symbolized by the Twins, Gemini is a positive, mutable, air sign. Thus, manner of thinking, speaking and writing aims for versatility, ingenuity, agility in expression of ideas. Intent is to dazzle opposition, to show the self as a quick-witted, dual-minded communicator. To some the swift leap-frogging from point to point is mentally amusing. To others, it is stressful, untrustworthy, feather-headed.

Behavioural keyword for Gemini: 'I think'. Thus Gemini talk runs on the 'I'm going to show you what kaleidoscopic thinking can do for you' track.

Mercury in Cancer. Symbolized by the Crab, Cancer is a negative, cardinal, water sign. Thus, manner of thinking, speaking and writing aims for intuitive, sensitive, emotionally slanted expression of ideas. Intent is to swamp opposition, to show the self as a tenacious, aware guardian of home and family. To some the responsive sharing of thoughts is mentally nourishing. To others, it is touchy, over-anxious, wet-blanketing.

Behavioural keyword for Cancer: 'I feel'. Thus Cancer talk runs on the 'Let's get a feel for what's going on here' track.

Mercury in Leo. Symbolized by the Lion, Leo is a positive, fixed, fire sign. Thus manner of thinking, speaking and writing aims for commanding, forceful, lordly expression of ideas. Intent is to over-rule opposition, to show the self as a broad-minded, benevolent dictator of ideas. To some the high-handed, heavy-footed ordering about is mentally vitalizing. To others, it is arrogant, self-appraising, flagrant.

Behavioural keyword for Leo: 'I will'. Thus Leo talk runs on 'We'll all do what *I* say!' track.

Mercury in Virgo. Symbolized by the Virgin, Virgo is a negative, mutable, earth sign. Thus, manner of thinking, speaking and writing aims for precise, detailed, discriminating expression of ideas. Intent is to take apart opposition, to show the self as a sensible, strict, inviolable critic. To some the puristic dissection of opinion is mentally intriguing. To others, it is narrow, fault-finding, tiresome.

Behavioural keyword for Virgo: 'I analyse'. Thus Virgo talk runs on the 'Let's take this idea to pieces first' track.

Mercury in Libra. Symbolized by the Scales, Libra is a positive, cardinal, air sign. Thus, manner of thinking, speaking and writing aims for intelligent, balanced, companionable expression of ideas. Intent is to disarm opposition, to show the self as a diplomatic, impartial arbitrator. To some the continual weighing up of pros and cons is mentally pleasing. To others, it is vacillating, overly rational, gutless.

Behavioural keyword for Libra: 'I judge'. Thus Libra talk runs on the 'Let's look at both these alternatives' track.

Mercury in Scorpio. Symbolized by the Scorpion, Scorpio is a negative, fixed, water sign. Thus, manner of thinking, speaking and writing aims for intense, penetrative, wary expression of ideas. Intent is to undermine opposition, to show the self as a watchful, subtle manipulator. To some the steady, observant stream of thought is strengthening. To others, it is harsh, extremist, stinging.

Behavioural keyword for Scorpio: 'I desire'. Thus Scorpio talk runs on the 'Nobody tells me what I want!' track.

Mercury in Sagittarius. Symbolized by the Centaur, Sagittarius is a positive, mutable fire sign. Thus, manner of thinking, speaking and writing aims for hearty, exuberant, far-seeing expression of ideas. Intent is to trample opposition, to show the self as an enthusiastic, all-round informant. To some the boisterous, tall-tale telling is energizing. To others, it is careless, baseless, slack.

Behavioural keyword for Sagittarius: 'I see'. Thus Sagittarian talk runs on the 'Wait till I tell you what I just spotted' track.

Mercury in Capricorn. Symbolized by the Goat, Capricorn is a negative, cardinal, earth sign. Thus, manner of thinking, speaking and writing aims for punctilious, well-ordered, pre-planned expression of ideas. Intent is to climb over opposition, to show the self as an ambitious, never-caught-unawares organizer. To some the sternly utilitarian lining up of thoughts is reassuring. To others, it is austere, depressive, deadening.

Behavioural keyword for Capricorn: 'I use'. Thus Capricorn talk runs on the 'Let's see what we can get out of this' track.

Mercury in Aquarius. Symbolized by the Water-Bearer, Aquarius is a positive, fixed, air sign. Thus, manner of thinking, speaking and writing aims for startling, original, free-wheeling expression of ideas. Intent is to outrage opposition, to show the self as an electrifying, future-oriented innovator. To some the wildly way-out direction of thought is exhilarating. To others, it is perverse, patronizing, bloody-minded.

Behavioural keyword for Aquarius: 'I know'. Thus Aquarian talk runs on the 'If you want to know which way the world's turning, ask me!' track.

Mercury in Pisces. Symbolized by the Fish, Pisces is a negative, mutable, water sign. Thus, manner of thinking, speaking and writing aims for imaginative, responsive, sympathetic expression of ideas. Intent is to flow over opposition, to show the self as an understanding, tuned-in inspirer. To some the meandering torrent of reflections is uplifting. To others, it is muddled, unrealistic, sloppy.

Behavioural keyword for Pisces: 'I believe'. Thus Pisces talks runs on the 'Let's believe in dreams this time and see where we finish up' track.

When assessing the Mercury-given ability to articulate and communicate in your own charts, don't forget (as noted in earlier chapters) to pay attention to the specific qualities of the Mercury signs you're handling — i.e. positive/negative, cardinal/mutable/fixed, fire/air/earth/water — but especially here the second-named.

● All *cardinal* signs exhibit a natural tendency to *co-ordinate*. According to their various modes of operation, each one of the four strives to co-ordinate mental energies on a given goal in a patently one-pointed manner. They push for their ends, overthrow opposition, driving themselves and others as relentlessly as football coaches (which is why they sometimes earn the unflattering label of 'go-getter thinkers').

● All *fixed* signs exhibit a natural tendency *to fixate*. According to their various modes of operation, each one of the four focuses mental energies on a given idea in an unmistakably immovable manner. No matter whether the idea is good or bad, advantageous or destructive, they stick with it like limpets on a rock (which is why they sometimes earn the unflattering label of 'die-hard thinkers').

● All *mutable* signs exhibit a tendency *to mutate*. According to their various modes of operation, each one of the four bends the mental energies this way and that in a visibly flexible manner. They change their thinking and ideas, alter their responses, take on the colour of the current scene as effortlessly as chameleons (which is why they sometimes earn the unflattering label of 'hypocritical thinkers').

Naturally, awkward Mercury links between partners do not mean their future together is a non-event. But these *do* mean it is far from being what Shakespeare called 'a marriage of true minds'. Mental peace will require frequent 'Summit Conferences!'

Remember in all talk situations, what one party *says* is not necessarily what the other party *hears*. The tone of voice used can be mistaken, anger/irritability can twist the meaning of the words in another's ears, smooth talk can simulate sincerity, clumsy expression can infer criticism not intended.

This danger is increased when you're dealing with 'disembodied' voices on the telephone. Without the physical presence of the other party, gestures, facial expression (which help reveal inner feelings) are not available to judge meaning by. Misunderstandings are hence given a flying start.

Test for yourself the effect of 'voice-minus-body' as against 'voice-plus-body' to gauge what a good or bad Mercury contact can do for you. Think of an occasion when you spoke on the telephone to someone you'd never met and then later confronted him/her in the flesh. If this individual's Mercury was well-placed and blended with your own, you would have almost certainly found his/her voice and manner of speaking attractive, and formed a favourable mental picture of its owner. If you discover on meeting that the physicals aren't up to scratch with the vocals, the let-down is doubly disappointing. You feel you've been tricked. And you have — by Mercury.

The Mercury effect works the other way round, too. Think of the small army of silent movie sex symbols who fell out of the screen world overnight when 'talking pictures' hit Hollywood. They had the right sort of looks but the wrong sort of sound. Sultry screen lover of the 1920s John Gilbert was a prime example of this. His voice reputedly recorded more like a strangled canary's than a sleek seducer's!

The same situation happens in everyday life too. No matter how appealing the physical self may be, a flat, unpleasant, unresponsive tone plus a dull way of talking is a Grade A turn-off. So if you're in the partner-picking business, listen to your own voice on a tape recorder and see if it's working for you or against you. Your Mercury patterns will further pinpoint what's right and what's wrong with it. What is appealing and what you need to improve.

Mercury Houses — Where the Mind Focuses

Since, as we saw earlier, Mercury's orbit is closest to the Sun, the planet will always be found near to the Sun in the natal chart, i.e. in the same house or one adjacent thereto. In previous chapters, we've looked at the influence of Mercury in those houses most concerned with love/romance (5th), home (4th) and marriage (7th). But what happens when you find the planet in houses which have little or nothing to do with these life sectors? In four short words — *the mind's working elsewhere*. Mercury will always apply himself most assiduously to the affairs of the house he occupies. To illustrate briefly:

- In the 1st, he's busy creating a witty, intellectual image.
- In the 2nd, he's figuring out how to make the most money.
- In the 3rd, he's throwing himself into studies and courses.
- In the 6th, he's impressing others in the work scene.
- In the 8th, he's juggling other people's monetary matters.
- In the 9th, he's polishing his philosophy through globe-trotting.
- In the 10th, he's speeding up career successes.
- In the 11th, he's gathering friends and joining groups.
- In the 12th, he's wondering how he can help lame dogs over styles.

Of course, the fact that Mercury occupies a less personal house or chart quadrant does not infer that the 'owner' of such a chart will never have marriage/relationships in mind. I think that situation is best interpreted by noting other interests/objectives absorb more mental energy.

Mercury Aspects — How the Mind Focuses

We haven't said much about Mercury's links with other planets up to this point as you'll find them discussed in detail in *How to Astro-Analyse Yourself and Others* or any other well-documented astrological text. However, we'll list some of the more significant ones hereunder from the standpoint of their effect on relationships.

Obviously, if Partner A's Mercury aspects help create a hard-line, abrasive talker/thinker and Partner B's create a soft, impressionable, tentative manner of expression, B is going to feel flattened — the more so if A is the female and B the male. He will feel unmanned, sound even more hesitant, or get up and go.

As before, we must blend in the interests of the house Mercury occupies for both parties, the signs of the planet for both, individual Mercury aspects and cross-referenced aspects in Man/Woman charts.

The special significance of the aspects is that they sharpen the impact of speech and writing — for better or worse.

Sun to Mercury (Will and Mentality)

Easy Aspects　= Own chart — in the natal chart itself, no aspect other than a conjunction or semi-sextile is possible as the two planets are never more than 28 degrees apart. Conjunctions blend ego and mind comfortably together. Semi-sextiles, as exemplified earlier, can bring in mental attitudes which do not quite fit with the ego's demands.

= Man/Woman charts — life goals of one are mentally acceptable to the other.

Hard Aspects = Man/Woman charts only: Troublesome. Reverse of above.

Moon to Mercury (Emotions and Mentality)
Easy Aspects = Own chart — better capacity to verbalize emotional needs.

= Man/Woman charts — mind of one responds well to emotions of the other.

Hard Aspects = Disintegrating. Reverse of above.

Venus to Mercury (Affections and Mentality)
Easy Aspects = Own chart — improved capacity for charm and pleasantness in communicating.

= Man/Woman charts — mind of one understands more easily affectional needs of the other.

Hard Aspects = Discomforting. Reverse of above.

Mars to Mercury See Chapter 3, Aspects section.

Mercury and the Heavy Planets
When Mercury links up with planets less closely associated with the personality's immediate structure — i.e. Saturn, Uranus, Neptune and Pluto — the effect on the individual is, in my experience, strong and unmistakable. However, cross links in man/woman charts between Mercury and the heavies do not seem to prop up or rattle the relationship (when we're looking for overall compatibility pointers) overly much. So we'll simply check through Mercury in hard aspect to the heavy planets in the individual natal chart. These aspects can play havoc with communication between partners because they create harsh, hurtful, nebulous or erratic thinking and speaking.

Keep all these points in the forefront of your mind if you're pondering why you and your partner are great in bed but can't really talk to each other. Disharmonious Mercury patterns are usually the culprits, either in own chart or cross-referenced man/woman charts.

Leading American psychologist/astrologer Stephen Arroyo, M.A., takes this point even further. He observes that when lecturing to classes, questions and answers often tangle themselves up in cases where his Mercury patterns clash with a particular student's. When the two Mercury patterns blend happily, he states, the most erudite discussion goes off without a hitch.

Thus we see that Mercury is not a planet to be taken lightly in compatibility. Inability to talk easily to each other, to exchange opinions confidently may seem a small matter at the outset of a relationship but not so later in the story. Not only will damaging arguments blot the union — differing ideas about money, children, extra-marital interests — but also neither partner will feel they're 'getting through'. They sense accurately that they are not talking *to* each other but *at* each other — a disappointing, alienating experience.

Mercury to Saturn
Hard Aspects = Individual charts only. Capable of brusque, hypercritical, overly conservative speech and thinking. Can create cold, cut-you-down-to-size utterances.

Mercury to Uranus
Hard Aspects = Individual charts only. Capable of opinionated, patronizing, erratic speech and writing. Can create brutally frank to-hell-with-tact utterances.

Mercury to Neptune
Hard Aspects = Individual charts only. Capable of confused thinking and self-deception. Can exhibit escapist tendencies when forced to face facts.

Mercury to Pluto
Hard Aspects = Individual charts only. Capable of fanatical, sarcastic, cynical speech and writing. Can create violent, tear-you-apart utterances.

Now, to see Mercury pointers at work in real life, let's tune in to the mental wavelengths of our specimen couple, Harry and Helen.

Mercury signs

Harry has his Mercury in the water sign of Scorpio. Helen has her Mercury in the air sign of Libra. Still, not much luck for these two. He's a non-verbal, wary communicator, keeps most of his ideas well under his hat, works on intuitive hunches.

She uses words well, is a diplomatic, companionable communicator, discounts hunches, works on reasoning things out. He found her easy to talk to when they met but soon began to resent the fact that so did everyone else. She feels that dragging an opinion from him on matters of importance belongs in the blood-out-of-a-stone category. Attempts at genuine exchange of ideas slowly sink into a sea of non-committal banalities.

Mercury houses

Harry has his Mercury in the 12th house. Helen has her Mercury in the 11th. His powers of communication are confined, trapped in the house of personal isolation/self-undoing. Hers are aimed at finding outlets through friends, with people of like minds in the house of socializing/group activities. He seethes because fellow guests at parties talk to her and ignore him. He solves the problem, Scorpio-style, by leaving her at home. The union slides slowly but surely towards the point of no return.

Fourteen years after they were married and six years before she left him, Helen's 11th house Libran Mercury made one last try for social harmony. She asked him to escort her to a prestigious formal ball at which she had to act as hostess to visiting dignitaries. Although then a greying, 43-year-old executive, he slouched into the ballroom in a hired dinner suit, *noisily chewing gum!* Highbrow eyebrows shot up to the chandeliers. Harry's 12th house Mercury in Scorpio had struck again, stinging Helen on her social soft-spot with devastating effect! By that act, he hammered the last nail into the coffin of communication and sharing of interests. It was the last time ever Helen invited Harry to go anywhere with her. All of which shows that Mercury can be just as much a marriage-wrecker as the tougher planets — when it suits him!

Mercury Aspects

Harry has Mercury in hard aspect to the Moon in the 4th house. Helen has Mercury in hard aspect to Pluto in the 7th house. When he talks to any female with whom he has personal ties, the words come out wrongly — a carry-over from childhood problems with his dominating mother. Helen, although normally diplomatic of speech, is capable of blood-curdling invective and outbursts of barely controlled fury when her opinions are challenged by the partner. On the rare occasions when she does slap him down, he feels like he's back in short pants, a chastised child. Both eventually decide the answer is to stop talking to each other. They do that. The last semblance of marriage ends. Uneasy and silent co-existence begins.

In listening to the tale of Harry and Helen in this and preceding chapters, you can see how the personality clashes and differences of opinion, which were inherent in the psychological make-up of both, gradually manifested themselves as the years passed — little by little, irritation by irritation, until there was nothing left but the words on the marriage certificate.

Theirs is not a cheering story but I chose it as an example of astro-analysis in action, because I knew them well and observed their progress over several years. And, because had their chart patterns been explained to them *when* they married, they could have stopped the slow rot which gradually destroyed their relationship. Their charts were not hopelessly hostile towards each other. (Few, in my experience, really are.) Molehills of disagreement could have stayed molehills instead of building up into mountains if Harry and Helen had only been shown — through their charts — where and when greater understanding of each other was needed. By the time I came in contact with them, the damage was done. It was all over bar the shouting.

Mercury Data at a Glance

Mercury's sign   Indicates natural manner of thought. Whether thinking is predominantly impulsive/enthusiastic (fire signs), predominantly rational/detached (air signs), predominantly cautious/practical (earth signs), or predominantly sensitive/intuitive (water signs).

Mercury's House   Reveals life sector upon which mind/intellect naturally focus. Mercury in houses linked to private affairs — love, marriage, home, children, shows mental as well as emotional interest in these areas. Mercury in houses linked to public affairs — career, money, education, work, travel — directs the mind away from emotional-type concerns.

Mercury's aspects   Act as channels for mental energy. Help or hamper its expression depending on whether the aspect is easy or hard for the total personality to accommodate.

Mercury patterns in Compatibility   Indicate how capable the partners are of communicating with each other and sharing common intellectual/leisure interests. Compatible Mercury patterns bring the two minds together. Incompatible Mercury patterns cause communication break-downs.

With Mercury to guide us, we've surveyed the landscape of the mind and observed how the planet can encourage us to talk our way into or out of trouble in our personal relationships.

Now, we're ready to take the final step before we begin to blend together in sample compatibility analyses, all the personality data we've been gathering. Through examining the impact of the twelve Ascendants, we'll see how the personality projects itself — that vital first *physical* impression we make on others.

Learning Sign Language from the Ascendant

Up till this chapter, we've looked mainly at the best ways and means of handling your relationships once they actually exist. But, how can you decide whether a new partner is right for you and sincerely interested during the initial skirmishes of a possible love affair? Those first words at a party? In a bar? On a plane? That first invitation to do something together? Do those things mean what they seem to mean? Or is it all pretence? Never easy questions to answer, of course. Especially when you realize that at this stage you're meeting not the true self of your latest interest but his/her Ascendant. Ascendant-style reactions are invariably the most obvious and all that most individuals see at first contact with a new acquaintance.

Every social situation demands a form of polite play-acting. The precise form these party manners take is dictated by everyone's Ascendant. That's why it is well worth taking the trouble to learn the visible characteristics and responses of the twelve possible Ascendants. Or — to sum it up in a phrase — to learn to understand 'sign language'. Then, you'll be in a better position to judge, if initial attraction develops into a relationship, how well the party play-acting matches up with the real person.

It is a well-established psychological fact that all kinds of gestures and movements — many of them involuntary — amount to unconscious body signals, indicating attraction to or rejection of a given person or situation.

The individual himself/herself is usually quite unaware of what their bodies are silently announcing to others. Thus these small and apparently insignificant actions reveal true feelings far more accurately than what is actually being said.

Gestures as ordinary as thrusting the thumbs downward into the belt can, for example, infer an unconscious assertion of virility on the part of males. If made towards another man, this gesture can suggest belligerence, an unstated desire for battle. If made towards a woman, it becomes provocative, a covert display of maleness by the thumbs pointing towards the sexual organs.

Shaking the head while agreeing verbally with what someone else is asserting is another common but revealing signal. The spoken words are denied by the gesture.

Early in a budding love affair, the way in which your new partner stands or sits — the hand, arm, facial movements, even the way the feet are pointed — offer valuable clues to what is really going on behind the eyes. As always, actions do speak louder than words! Hence, although the lips can be mouthing several varieties of classic brush-offs from — 'Well, actually I'm booked every night next week', all along the line to — 'I'm not into relationships' — the body posture, the gestures can be contradicting every word.

If you find yourself in this scene and you've interpreted the signals correctly, you're looking at the 'green light', disguised as a 'red light'. Possibilities are promising. Conversely, you can find yourself faced with positive verbal statements, covering up negative bodily statements. This time you're looking at the 'red light', masquerading as a 'green light'. Possibilities are poor.

In psychological studies, assessment of response by these kinds of physical signals is termed 'body language'. In astro-analytical studies, we'll term it 'sign language' since each sign exhibits recognizable physical characteristics and modes of behaviour. Gestures and body movements which bespeak a forceful, confident, overtly physical approach or those which imply a tentative, subtle, shy, even nervous advance.

Broadly speaking, the former type are more common with fire or air well-emphasized in a chart and through a fire or air Ascendant. The latter type usually stem from water or earth dominant in a chart and through water or earth Ascendants.

Another intriguing pointer to watch for is the often startling effect of a positive sign rising over negative Sun and/or Moon Signs. (As you'll recall all the fire and air signs are positive; all the earth and water signs are negative.)

Positive signs are by their very nature more immediately reactive, more people-oriented, more extroverted. Thus they handle social situations more easily and comfortably than do the negatives.

Yet, when you run up against an individual with either a fire or air Ascendant, sitting on top — as it were — of an earth or water Sun sign, you're usually looking at a contradiction in terms: someone who *appears* to all intents and purposes to be an 'All-Night Rager' but is the next best thing to a hermit underneath. The opposite effect results when negative signs are rising over positive signs.

The simplest way to remember this pointer is to use a homespun analogy and imagine each human type as a cake.

● The decorative icing on top stands for the Ascendant — the Projected Personality.
● The baked cake itself stands for the Sun Sign — the True Self.
● The blended ingredients stand for the Moon Sign — the Instinctive Responses.

Since there are hundreds of varieties of icings, cakes and ingredients, this mental picture will serve to remind you of the equally numerous mixes of personality traits. In some individuals, the 'icing' is so brightly coloured, so skilfully whipped and moulded, you're positively shocked when you cut through to a heavy, even soggy cake, full of tough-looking nuts. Or, to take it the other way round. The 'icing' may look pretty unappealing yet beneath the surface, the 'flavour' is enticing. Or, again, you may strike a personality blend that's so mixed up, it's as if somebody lost the recipe book.

The foregoing analogy is of especial importance when you're

considering the initial impact of one personality on another at first meeting, since social behaviour derives largely from the individual blend of Ascendant, Sun and Moon Sign traits.

As our analogy demonstrates these three influences may mix easily together, thereby creating a more cohesive, smoother impact. Or, they may conflict wildly, thereby creating a quite confusing, disconcerting impact.

Those 'green-masquerading-as-red-light' situations described earlier invariably result from the latter. They happen when the Ascendant is willing to leap into a love affair but the Sun and/or Moon signs baulk at the whole idea.

Bear in mind always (as noted earlier) that the Ascendant decides *how we wish others to see us*. The part of ourselves that we project and put on show because that is how we feel we ought to be. However, except in cases where both Ascendant and Sun are in the same sign, the projected personality remains no more than an overlay and does not exhibit the traits of the true self.

To illustrate: A 38-year-old professional man whose chart I analysed some ten years ago had a Scorpio Ascendant which had convinced him he could be a Great Lover to the point he secretly saw himself in that role. But he had a Pisces Sun and a Taurus Moon. And he was married to a Libran with a Pisces Ascendant. (Attractions between the Ascendant of one partner and the Sun Sign of the other are common but do not augur well for compatibility where more significant chart patterns conflict, as they did in this case.) Thus he was sexually and emotionally frustrated, looking around for new turn-ons. One morning he rang me, bursting with excitement. A Scorpio man friend of his had just told him the secret of bedding any woman he wanted — instantly!

'It's simple,' the Scorpion had said. 'All you do is pick your target for the night at a party, walk up, pin her to the wall and state what you intend, using the one unmistakeable four-letter word.'

The impressionable Piscean was all set to do just that until I warned him against it. Agreed, he looked Scorpionic — dark, heavily built, sharp arrowhead brows, intense eyes — but the resemblance ended at the superficial level of the Ascendant. He did not have the uncompromising sexual magnetism of the Sun Scorpio and thus could never have got away with such a brutally direct approach.

Ascendant traits are really only 'skin-deep'. Although his own might have been strong enough to propel him into trying out the ploy, his romantic Piscean Sun and affectionate Taurean Moon would have refused to play and turned the performance into a farce.

That short story demonstrates why it's so important to recognize the 'vibe' of each Ascendant, which will not only allow you to tune in to it better but also offer foreknowledge of how its 'owner' will present in most social situations.

Interpretations of Ascending Signs

Way back in 1942, American astrologer Charles E. Luntz formulated a lengthy list of Ascendant-style reactions in his book, *Vocational Guidance by Astrology*. In my view, these are keenly observed and well described and although they were specifically intended for use in personnel selection, they are equally valid for partner choices. Here follow some brief excerpts of Luntz's pointers, together with some of my own observations on how to recognize each Ascendant.

Fire signs rising, i.e. Aries the Ram, Leo the Lion, Sagittarius the Centaur: Initial impression of physical vigour, animal magnetism, bright and shiny eyes. Usually direct and full on in making or responding to a 'pass'. Acts first, thinks second. Appears confident.

Luntz adds for Aries: Abrupt, impatient manner. Likes to order others about. Projects put over in a rush.

For Leo: Frank, open manner. Very trustworthy, seldom dishonest. Rules rather than leads. Condescends to subordinates.

For Sagittarius: Often very tall. Appears athletic. Does best when full trust is placed upon him/her.

Air signs rising, i.e. Gemini the Twins, Libra the Scales, Aquarius the Water-Bearer. Initial impression of intelligence, lightness and social ease, being though sometimes airily argumentative. Usually flirtatious and talkative in making or responding to a 'pass'. Spends more time chatting up a prospect instead of closing in.

Luntz adds for Gemini: Very dexterous. Born 'wisecracker'. Good mentality but divided energies. Not strong on method but very good improviser.

For Libra: Particular about personal appearance. Very good judgement and artistic sense. Humane in personal contacts.

For Aquarius: Good-looking, friendly, very up-to-date. Decisive, intelligent workers but would rather play. Often shows all-round ability.

Earth signs rising, i.e. Taurus the Bull, Virgo the Virgin, Capricorn the Goat. Initial impression of steadiness, matter-of-fact attitudes, reliability. Usually slower and more cautious in making or responding to a 'pass'. Looks for clear sign of reciprocal interest before moving. Appears responsible.

Luntz adds for Taurus: Bulldog tenacity, equable temperament unless aroused. Not an originator but carries out ideas well.

For Virgo: Follows others with eyes. Finicky about food, faddy about health. Best detail worker but dislikes making decisions.

For Capricorn: Suspicious expression. Great worriers and easily irritated. Good executive types but not too easy to get along with.

Water signs rising, i.e. Cancer the Crab, Scorpio the Scorpion, Pisces the Fish. Initial impression of vulnerability, emotional sensitivity and being visibly reactive to atmosphere. Usually indirect and non-verbal in making or responding to a 'pass'. Feels out the scene, relying on hunches and intuition. Appears wary.

Luntz adds for Cancer: Very sensitive and homeloving. Dislikes scenes and demands respect. Tenacious and apparently self-assured.

For Scorpio: Formidable appearance, undaunted fighters with enormous staying power. Excellent for difficult or dangerous missions.

For Pisces. Very philosophical in misfortune. Good-looking in a dreamy way. Often highly creative imagination.

Remember, of course, when applying the above to friends or associates that no single individual will exhibit all the characteristic traits of a given sign. Planets in or near the Ascendant have a marked effect on physical attributes as do numerous other factors in the horoscope chart.

Nevertheless, if you keep track of these specific indicators and really learn this special kind of Sign Language, you'll find Ascendants become a lot easier to pick!

Take careful note of them, especially when you're planning to dash into a new relationship. If you've fallen madly in love with your prospective partner's Ascendant and later discover it was only an assumed mask, you're going to wake up one morning sadder and (hopefully) wiser.

I can personally speak from experience on that matter. In my twenties, well after I qualified as a psychologist but long before I had qualified as an astro-analyst, I made the Ascendant mistake in love affairs twice!

In the first relationship, I found I luckily loved his Sun and Moon Sign traits as much as those of his contrary Ascendant so all would have augured well for our future together had he not died suddenly when we were both very young. The second relationship revealed later that I couldn't handle his Sun and Moon signs at all and he couldn't handle mine. We'd both been attracted by our respective Ascendants only. Result? Endless gnashing of teeth on both sides!

At the times I became involved with these two men, I remember thinking my training as a psychologist should have indicated both 'plain sailing' and 'danger' zones in relating to them. But it did not! Only painstaking astro-analysis is capable of achieving a clear-cut picture of compatibility or lack of it — as I discovered when I erected their charts some twenty years after the events had taken place.

So, do remember, in either your business or private relationships, the old saying 'All that glitters is not gold'. Until you come to know your associates well, your opinion will be chiefly based on their Ascendants. And underneath a glittering surface, you may well find a grab-bag of traits that are heavy as lead!

Readers well-experienced in astrological calculation will naturally be fully aware of methods used to ascertain the correct Ascendant for each individual chart. However, for those readers who are newcomers to astrological science, the following information will prove helpful. Unless you know the *precise* time of day at which the birth occurred, the Ascendant cannot be calculated. But many people do not know or are very vague on that vital question so let's see what can be done when the time is unknown or uncertain.

The Problem of the Unknown Birth-Time

'I'm adopted so nobody knows when I was born' . . . 'My parents are both dead so I've no way of finding out now!' . . . 'My mother won't tell me because she doesn't believe in astrology!'

The above forlorn cries are familiar to every practitioner, including me, but I have been quite surprised to learn lately that many laymen are totally unaware that unknown or uncertain birth-times can be discovered by process of deduction known as 'rectification'. Basically, this works by checking back through past events and relationships in an individual's life. If carried out by a qualified and experienced practitioner, it gives an accurate answer as to birth-time.

So don't despair if you're an Unknown Birth-Timer yourself and decide there's no chance of your ever having an accurate and complete chart erected for you. The puzzle *can* be solved!

But while we're on the birth-time subject, here are a few pointers.

1. Most major hospitals keep records, some going back more than forty years, and suppy birth-time data if requested. Some charge a fee to search their records; some don't.
2. Some adopting parents are furnished with details of their chosen child's birth-time.
3. If parents are deceased, some other family members may recall an approximate time which, if reliable, can be used as a starting-point.
4. In cases where mother refuses to tell because she 'doesn't believe in astrology', I usually ask: 'How many years has your mother devoted to the study of astrological science to arrive at this state of disbelief?' At this point, there is generally what romantic novelists used to describe as a 'pregnant pause', followed by: 'Oh, well. That is . . . I don't think Mother knows anything about astrology at all. She just . . . well, she just says she doesn't believe in it!'

Q.E.D. as Euclid would have said. (The thing has been proved.) Sad, though, that in this enlightened age astrology still has to fight so hard against such a tacky mixture of ignorance and prejudice. Fear, too. Some types of people are afraid to learn the truth about themselves and their own motivations, because they *might* have to try to do something about changing themselves — which is, doubtless, why astrology is so often in somebody's firing-line. After all, few laymen understand Einstein's theory of relativity and have no more than the vaguest notion of what it is all about. But who would dare to say 'they didn't believe in relativity!' Not a single soul!

Watch out for 'Ascendo-Mania'

Although in the latter half of this chapter I've concentrated on Ascendants plus the style of behaviour and physical attributes they dictate, their significance must not be allowed to dominate your thinking on compatibility questions. Moreover, I've lately observed that side by side with escalating public interest in astrological science, there's been an obvious outbreak of what I term 'Ascendo-mania'. Or to phrase it another way, this means fixating on Ascendants to the point that the rest of the personality data contained in the horoscope chart is virtually ignored.

This fixation is quite common among beginners — a little knowledge is a dangerous thing! So I think a few quick comments here on Ascendant calculation will help to put the whole personality picture in better perspective.

We'll illustrate the problem with three capsule case histories of 'ascendo-mania' in action. All of them actually happened.

Burning Ascendo-Mania

Client consulted one well-known astrologer and didn't like the Ascendant calculated. Consulted an unknown practitioner, whose calculations came up with a different Ascendant. Client promptly *burnt* the first chart on the second astrologer's advice. Client then again consulted first astrologer, gaily stating she had destroyed the chart because 'it was all wrong'.

Comment: Different methods of calculation can give slightly differing Ascendants, either by sign or by degree or both. In above example, it is possible that this occurred or that a mistake had been made by either astrologer, such as failure to check 'Daylight Saving' time. The fact that this client did not like the Ascendant in the first instance is, however, an indication that this was the correct one. Psychologically speaking, some personalities attempt to repress or brush under the carpet parts of themselves they don't want to accept.

In any event, the Ascendant has little or no effect on many other important factors in the horoscope chart — signs planets occupy, planetary aspects, etc. This little tale also illustrates the danger of shopping around from one practitioner to another. If you do that you can become hopelessly confused by different interpretative styles and chart construction methods — and maybe, find yourself in the burning-off business too!

Graphic Ascendo-Mania

Client rang his astrologer and announced he'd been assigned the wrong Ascendant because he's just bought a popular astrology book containing a 'Find Your Ascendant' graph.

Comment: Never, never use Ascendant Graphs or Tables published in even the better-class astrology texts except as the most general of guidelines. These graphs or tables have to be averaged in any case to cover every possible birth-time, but usually divide the twenty-four hours of each day into two-hour birth-time groups.

Thus factors like Daylight Saving, Sign Interception, etc. are not allowed for. The net result therefore is that the graph or table can be quite wrong. Hence if your chart has been calculated by a competent astrologer, the Ascendant assigned to you will be right — even if it does not agree with graphs or tables in textbooks.

Decanating Ascendo-Mania

Client ordered charts at the same time from two experienced astrologers. The charts looked much the same except that the degree of the Ascendant was three degrees higher in one. Client became instantly agitated and wanted to set up a sort of Royal Commission to find out which astrologer was right, also assuming that the above-mentioned three degrees would mean the difference between a chart that was 'totally wrong or totally right'.

Comment: Each sign of the zodiac is divided into sets of ten degrees and thus are called 'decanates'. In the above circumstances, the first chart showed the Ascendant in the first decanate of the appropriate sign whereas the second chart showed it in the second decanate.

Some authoritative textbooks place great emphasis on the decanates for specific types of interpretation and forecasting, others pay scant attention to this point. I would surmise that the problem here arose from the use of different Tables of Houses or other reference works. Both astrologers would therefore have been right. And neither chart, in any case, would provide 'totally wrong' data.

From these examples, you will observe that some individuals overreact to the point of near hysteria when trying to understand themselves and their charts — the more so if they've picked up a scrappy idea of astrology beforehand. Be on guard for this in circumstances where you may wish to counsel others on compatibility questions.

You do run across cases where individuals subconsciously reject the Ascendant characteristics as in (1) above. This results in an attempt to repress all of the needs and behavioural traits of the Ascendant and, in extreme cases, can lead to neuroses. Like murder, the Ascendant will out. It is an integral and important part of the total 'You'.

Quick-reference check-points

Plus or Minus Indicators of Mental Compatibility and Initial Attraction

Mercury Mismatches: When your own Mercury is well-placed and aspected, step warily if your intended's is not. Communication will assuredly break down somewhere along the line because you'll be thinking rationally and he/she will not.

A troubled Mercury can create a stack of problems from a one-track mentality to fantasy-style thinking; e.g. One highly intelligent 29-year-old woman actually accepted her partner's statement that he did not enjoy sex because in a previous life he had taken a vow of celibacy! (Two cases of troubled Mercurys here.)

Another 41-year-old executive told his lover he could never leave his wife and children and thus they must part for ever. But he said he adored her (the lover) so much that he would send his thoughts and dreams to her telepathically each day so that they could live together in spirit till the end of their lives. Fifteen months later he divorced his wife, left his children and married a teenager. (Here, luckily, the lover's Mercury was both rational and realistic. She perceived at once he had taken up residence on Fantasy Island as events soon proved.)

There literally is no end to the delusions and convolutions in thinking that troubled Mercurys can instigate.

Note: Two immensely significant life-changing planetary transits happen to everyone around the ages of 29 (Case 1) and 40 (Case 2). These will be treated at length in my next book, on Future Life Trend Forecasting.

Family tune-ins: In talking to a wide cross-section of people interested in astrology (seriously interested, not dabbling), I've observed that nearly all have some family background that drew them towards the science. Often, it may be as far back as a grandparent; e.g. Nostradamus' grandfather was an expert astrologer and it was he who first encouraged the embryonic prophet to study horoscopes while still little more than a child.

So, have a check around in your family ancestry and see if one or more among your forebears set your feet upon the path.

You'll usually find compatible Mercury patterns with a close relative tuned you in to astrological thinking. With me, it was mainly my Aquarian mother. She only knew a little about astrology but she did have a 'feel' for Sun signs and very often guessed them correctly. (And that was at a time when astrology was an uncommon rather than an almost universal interest.)

Culture transplants: Since jet air travel turned the world into a global village, inter-marriage and pairings between couples of hugely differing cultures and social backgrounds have become an everyday occurrence. But there's no doubt they put further pressure on relationships — particularly if the pair meet in the country of one and settle in the country of the other.

Naturally, several chart factors bear on the success or otherwise of the union in the long-term, although a study of the Mercury patterns of both will indicate if the mental flexibility to handle drastic changes in thinking and lifestyle exists.

This situation requires even more careful deliberation where the spoken language of both countries is the same, e.g. Britain, America, Australia, New Zealand, South Africa, Canada. Being a natural-born Australian myself, I have noted this problem particularly where British men or women have married Australians and migrated here. Many seem to have believed that this country was a kind of South Pacific England. Nothing could be farther from the truth!

It's worth noting for those who may contemplate living in Australia that the whole place has a Sagittarian 'flavour', summed up in that famous phrase (which covers every problem from a broken heart to a leaking drain pipe) — 'She'll be right, mate!' Which, translated, means: 'Why worry me or yourself about anything? It'll all work out in the end.'

If you're from Britain or Europe and your Mercury patterns are affronted by this attitude, life here won't be too easy; e.g. A young English couple migrated to Sydney, but two years later the husband left the wife for an Australian girl, saying 'She makes me feel at home here. You never left England.' Sadly, this was true. The husband's Mercury and other chart patterns had adapted quickly. The wife's Mercury in the home-and-country sign of Cancer had refused to be transplanted into alien soil.

Even more telling is the following statement by a 30-year-old German who had lived in Australia since infancy: 'I'll never understand your lot,' said he. 'You're all white boongs!' ('Boong' is derogatory local slang for aboriginals or Pacific islanders, neither of which group are work-oriented in the European sense.) Again this was largely a Mercury in Cancer response which had made him see Australians as shiftless, careless work-dodgers. Even though he had never lived in Germany, his Mercury had stayed where he was born and refused to budge.

So never underestimate the power of the mind if you're thinking of teaming up with a foreigner and/or living in a new country.

Coping with Cusp Ascendants: The problem of a 'Cusp Ascendant' — that is, when the degree of the rising sign is close to the sign immediately preceding or following it — has often been the subject of learned debate and controversy. Some authors maintain that even if your Ascendant is 0 degrees 26 minutes of Capricorn, for example, you're a Capricorn rising type. Others say the influence here of adjacent Sagittarius has to be considered. Others again suggest your personality will press more towards the expression of Capricorn characteristics if the rest of your chart indicators show a predominance of earth. Or, more towards Sagittarius if you have a predominance of fire. (Remember, Capricorn is an earth sign; Sagittarius is a fire sign.)

Even more controversy exists as to the precise number of degrees which should be allowed when deciding if the Ascendant is on a cusp. Personally, I think consideration of the effect of an adjacent sign is always wise when the degree of any Ascendant is anything from 28 degrees of one sign and two degrees of the next.

Ascendant v. Sun and Moon: When discussing this point with students, I often liken the Ascendant to a channel or pipe through which the true self (your Sun Sign) must flow in its attempts to express its traits. If that channel and the surface level characteristics it implies blend happily with the Sun and also Moon Signs, nothing blocks the flow of expression, and the overall personality impact is comfortably cohesive. On the other hand, if the Ascendant dictates behaviour at odds with the Sun and/or Moon Signs, the flow of expression may be blocked or diverted into startlingly contrary behaviour.

Remember, Ascendant-style reactions are what most of us see when we first meet a new acquaintance. The impact on us may be pleasing or the reverse — depending on how easily our own Ascendant, Sun, Moon patterns respond to such impact.

But don't forget, as leading English textbook author Jeff Mayo put it

when discussing the role of the Ascendant on p. 93 of *Teach Yourself Astrology*: 'It can be the face a man wears whilst he projects himself into his business and social activities, concealing much of his true character that only intimates — and often not even they — know exists.'

Romance — Ascendant plus Sun Style: The Ascendant/Sun blend can produce some sudden turnabouts when it comes to love and sex — as these two amusing tales from my personal casebook illustrate:

1. Male: Sagittarian Ascendant + Sagittarian Sun: It's a rare thing to find a typical Centaur crying in his oats over a lost love or pressing a faded rose into his diary with a trembling hoof. But I thought for a moment I had at last come across this legendary creature on the other end of my telephone a few months ago. I had known this particular Centaur as a friend and client for several years and he was relating to me at great length the tragic tale of his latest filly having bolted from the home stable.

Finally he sobbed; 'That's it! I'm finished! A man might as well go and jump off a cliff!' (This last was accompanied by a faint, chomping sound.)

'Oh, I quite sure you won't do that,' I replied.

The chomping sound suddenly ceased.

'No,' he said with a quick change of tone. 'Can you hang on a sec while I go and find another piece of chocolate?'

All of which goes to show that when both Ascendant and Sun Sign work comfortably together in fire signs, crying over broken hearts doesn't last long. I suspect this particular Centaur would have been far more genuinely anguished if he'd broken a tooth!

2. Male: Virgo Ascendant + Leo Sun: Lion personalities very often *do* have a look of the big cats about them and this handsome specimen padded down my hall, flung his mane back and struck a suitably dramatic pose as he curled up on a chair.

'I have a *terrible* problem,' he growled, '*Terrible!*'

'Oh,' said I. 'What is it?'

His moustache twitched (just like whiskers), and his expression became more heart-rending by the moment.

'Women,' he said after a heavy pause. 'Women keep dragging me into bed. What can I do about it?'

I was tempted to say: 'Nothing. Just enjoy it'. But looking at the lighter side of love problems is rarely the Lion's forte. Just like the real lion, they prefer to pair-bond for life and rush frantically for their dens if pounced upon by too many females at once.

In this instance, of course, his prissy, puristic Virgo ascendant had added to the Lion's worries. Muttering ceaselessly inside his head about the wages of sin and the virtues of unremitting industry, relating in graphic detail the evils which befell all who gave way to the temptations of the flesh, the Ascendant had come close to destroying this Leo's natural capacity for loving.

As I have pointed out earlier, the Ascendant, Sun and Moon signs resemble three different personalities — all living together in the same body. Each must be allowed to express itself, or trouble follows — real trouble.

A Last Look at Harry and Helen

Before we say farewell to our specimen couple, let's check and see if the Ascendant— Sun — Moon comparisons have added a new twist to their story. Yes, they have thickened the plot but again not too hopefully.

Air-type Harry has a water Ascendant, air Sun and air Moon; Earth-type Helen has a fire Ascendant, earth Sun and earth Moon. Being airy, Harry is attracted by fire and was roped in by Helen's Ascendant. On the other hand, earthy Helen feels pulled towards water and was hooked by Harry's Ascendant.

They married after a very brief acquaintance, before either had seen past the masking effect of their two Ascendants. Result? He mistakenly thought she was fiery and exciting, a life-of-the-party type. She wrongly thought he was deep and emotional, a caring shoulder to cry on in times of trouble.

Two years later (it can take that long, or longer) their true selves emerged from behind their Ascendants. Her matter-of-fact earthy lifestyle bored him stiff. His endless socializing drove her to screaming point. Everytime he poured another beer for party stragglers at four in the morning, she barely restrained herself from breaking the bottle over his head. Yet they stayed married for more than twenty years. Why? Why did *they*? Why does anyone?

The answer to that question (and many other curly ones) is to be found from detailed cross-referencing of any two charts. And that's exactly what we'll learn to do in the next and final chapter.

CHAPTER SIX

Putting Yourselves Together

The Man-Woman Synthesis

We've looked at love from both sides now — as a sixties pop song once put it. From up and down, from win or lose, and we can now see the whole damn thing is not quite as impenetrably mysterious as it first appeared. Like Ariadne of the Greek myths, the natal chart always offers you 'the silken thread' that — provided you never lose your grip on it — will lead you out of the labyrinth of hopes/fears, emotions/drives that largely explain why you fall for and maybe marry a certain partner at a certain time. How skilfully you wind together those silken threads will determine the outcome. Whether you'll one day be sitting together in the twilight, remembering the first smile, the first kiss. Or the first time you thought of slipping arsenic in the breakfast coffee.

As with all human relationships, the end of love is in the beginning. If *your* love affair started off on the wrong foot, it will almost certainly end that way. Unless . . unless you both care enough to change your ways. To apply the knowledge of yourself and your partner the two blended charts provide. In short, to take the good with the bad.

It virtually goes without saying that no union is perfect, even though the couple themselves may believe so. Love and happy marriages survive the onslaught of time because both partners have worked towards this end. There has been genuine give-and-take, genuine tolerance, genuine sharing. Often these qualities have been painfully learned through trial and error. Less often, they came naturally because the pair were from the outset the proverbial 'perfect match'.

There is no doubt that some individuals instinctively follow the pull of their natal charts without consciously knowing the planetary patterns shown therein. American vocational guidance consultant Charles E.

Luntz demonstrated this many times through the charts of U.S. multi-millionaires, citing particularly the case of the first Rockefeller, whose powerfully placed natal Neptune literally pitch-forked him into the then budding oil industry and raised him from a lowly clerk to one of the richest men in the world.

Luntz states that people like Rockefeller sense instinctively where their natal talents lie and without a moment's doubt or hesitation put them to work. (Being born under Cancer, John. D. Rockefeller applied his with the co-ordinated thrust of the cardinal sign.)

The same instinctive pull draws others inexorably towards the right partner but that happy state is the exception rather than the rule. Less fortunate characters like you and me have to make use of every scrap of the help we can get to forestall misunderstandings, avoid wrong moves, quieten clashing egos and sidestep the myriad other mistakes that bedevil the average union.

We can do all that by living through and learning from the parade of possible miseries — which is the hard way. Or we can work on the theory that prevention is better than cure by using the natal charts to stop troubles *before* they happen — which is the easy and much faster way.

When you meticulously cross-reference your chart with your partner's, the clash-points and soft-spots stand out like beacons on a black night. In that manner, it allows you to take a short-cut to mutual understanding that might otherwise have taken years to acquire, or have caused the love affair to crash in flames before it really got off the ground. I should stress at this point, however, that it takes two to do it. You can change yourself *if* you really want to but you cannot change any other person. That's his/her job. If you alone are determined to use the charts to change your bed of thorns into a bed of roses, you'll succeed up to a point but not all along the line. The partner must be at least willing to try within the limits of his/her natal potentials or the effort becomes all one-way and so both demanding and discouraging.

Still, any sincere attempt at better understanding by one partner usually involves a warmer response by the other, which, if continued caringly, will begin to bridge even the deepest chasms. That does not mean, of course, you can turn a hopeless relationship into a heavenly one by hoping and trying. If the charts show a particular person is totally wrong for you and does not belong in your scene, nothing you can do will alter the result. Best to give up now while you're still in one piece and look elsewhere.

Many are the times when I've been approached by desperate, deserted lovers/spouses who've sought the charts of their lost loves to find out how to get them back. In cases where the break is so absolute that even a child could see it, I always tell the deserted it is a waste of time and money. Painful as it is to let go of someone you love, if the other is through with you, that very hard fact must be accepted. There is no more point in crying over split heart's blood than there is over spilt milk: an important thought to remember when you're counselling clients or friends on relationships.

I often think of two cases of two different males which illustrate this situation. Both were in their early fifties: both had lived for several years with much younger women: both had been told 'it was over' in no uncertain manner. One of them even admitted his ex-partner had left him three years earlier, had married a man of her own age and become the mother of two children.

Former friends of both had told the deserted partner she was obviously very happy and never mentioned him in any way. Yet he was still nurturing the fantasy that one day she would realize the error of her ways and come back to him. How blind love is! I told him he would be much wiser to learn to understand his own chart so that he could begin to bury the past and look for someone else.

However, there is one important item of self-knowledge that can be learned from a broken long-term relationship, i.e. its effect in changing the two participants. I had once thought this was a self-evident fact which everyone would realize, but years of counselling have proved to me otherwise. Now, whenever a client approaches me for advice concerning relationships, I always ask them for the birth data of any previous spouses or *de facto* partnerships.

Many clients appear surprised. As one 40-year-old female put it: 'What's my ex-husband got to do with my present lover? My last marriage is ancient history.' It isn't, of course. Long-term cohabitation with the right or wrong partner changes both individuals. Through the eyes and actions of the other, we are forced to see ourselves differently. And we are forced through whatever ups and downs we've experienced in permanent unions, to view relationships differently. We are no longer starry-eyed about them. Maybe, even a little hard-eyed. Just as the conditioning of our parents can direct our actions and thoughts long after both are dead, so will the conditioning of former partners affect us long after they are dead too — physically or metaphorically.

If the past pairing was pretty catastrophic, we have the scars to show for it and worse, may saddle the new lover with the faults of the old. If our past pairing was close to idyllic and ended in the death of the loved person, we can find ourselves in the perilous situation of extolling the virtues of the dead at the expense of the living. Thus it is wise to look to the basic chart patterns of the past lovers when comparing your own with a new partner. The chart may show, for example, you were required to experience and learn from one mistake in order to make you a better mate next time around.

Important Note

Don't read through the compatibility ratings in this chapter as if they had no practical application outside the lives of our test couples. Problems in love/marriage are rarely unique. Keep your own charts handy on your desk as you study our examples, marking down pointers relevant to you and yours, similar clash or compatibility patterns, similar upsets and how they were or weren't solved by the participants. In this manner, you'll be putting your knowledge to a practical test and building a compatibility rating dossier for yourselves as you go.

Solar Compatibility Rating

We use the simplest method first — Solar Chart Compatibility Rating. This is very handy for a quick, preliminary check on compatibility with anyone you care about or with those who have a significant role in your life, such as friends, family, bosses, etc.

Solar Compatibility Rating requires only the dates and years of birth of your subjects plus access to a planetary ephemeris. There is no calculation work or chart construction required. Birth times are not used in this method either, so it does not require consideration of Ascendants, house cusps or planetary house positions.

Thus Solar Compatibility Rating is *very easy* for beginners in astro-analysis to cut their teeth on. Naturally, it is nothing like as detailed and comprehensive as the comparison of two fully erected charts which we'll set about later in this chapter. Yet it never fails to give spot-on clues as to each relationship's 'Yes's' and 'No's', 'If's' and 'But's', plus valuable insight into the individual personalities of anyone important to you.

However, unless you're certain you have the right birthdate and the right year, watch out for a spot of white-lying, especially if your subject has teamed up with a much younger partner. One of my clients had asked me for a Solar Compatibility Rating with her new husband. She was 28 and said he was 51. I had previously met the man and the chart patterns for his stated date plus year of birth did not fit him at all. I told his wife this. Later she rang me — not a little shaken. At a well-wined dinner party the previous night, her husband had suddenly begun telling tall tales of his World War II adventures. At this, a fellow guest (his brother-in-law) remarked such feats were even more astounding since their hero must have been the only 14-year-old bomber pilot in the R.A.A.F.

Lying about one's age is ever a perilous undertaking. This man had knocked a seven-year chunk off his, rearranged his birthdate but had forgotten to rearrange his history!

In all examples considered in this chapter, we'll be dealing with real people. Names and identifying details have of course been changed to ensure there is no infringement of confidentiality.

Case No. 1: Dick and Jenny

Dick was born on 27 February 1949. He is a commercial artist, divorced with one child, who is in its mother's care and custody. Jenny was born on 29 January 1953. She is single, a part-time actress and model. She is seriously thinking of marrying Dick.

Below on the rating table form, you'll see listed the positions of the five personal planets, taken directly from a noon ephemeris, for the respective birthdates of Dick and Jenny.

Please take care to note the following whenever you prepare Solar Compatibility Rating Tables:

1. As this method does not use fully erected birth charts based on birth-times, planetary positions are simply written down in round figures from the ephemeris.
2. If a planet is right on the cusp of a sign, e.g. 0.12 Virgo or 29.30 Capricorn, allow for the influence of the adjacent sign: Leo for the Virgo example; Aquarius for the Capricorn example.

3. Since the Moon moves so swiftly it can change signs from one day to the next, it is always wise to allow for some influence from the adjacent sign if the Moon position as shown in the ephemeris is within 5 degrees of a cusp, especially in Southern Hemisphere births.
4. The Elemental Stress Patterns and other categories are listed by checking all ten planets, again from the ephemeris. The sign of each planet denotes its element and its category.
5. Always assign in (4) an extra point to Sun and Moon because of the dominating role the ego and the emotions play in personality projection.
6. In this book, we consider compatibility pointers chiefly as to their role in love/marriage partnerships. If you're looking at business or professional partnerships, planets other than the personal ones must also be assessed in the subjects' charts first and then both sets compared, so that direction of personal ambitions, use of business opportunities, etc., can be examined. Interpretations of the five non-personal planets — Jupiter through to Pluto — their signs, house positions and aspects are fully set out in *How To Astro-Analyse Yourself and Others.*

(Incidentally, if you don't understand at once how specific conclusions are reached with regard to each personality in all the analyses set out in the following pages, please re-read appropriate sections in preceding chapters.)

Preliminary Observations on Man-woman Synthesis: Dick and Jenny
We see merely from checking the ephemeris that the couple's personal planets are in these signs:

Dick			*Jenny*		
Sun	—	Pisces	Sun	—	Aquarius
Moon	—	Pisces	Moon	—	Leo
Mercury	—	Aquarius	Mercury	—	Aquarius
Venus	—	Aquarius	Venus	—	Pisces
Mars	—	Pisces	Mars	—	Pisces

So, what conclusions about this pair can we draw at first glance? Emphasis and cross-emphasis on the signs of Aquarius and Pisces for starters, showing similarities of behaviour but at different response levels.

Obviously, both members of our test couple are personally *and* interpersonally involved in a similar struggle between the dictates of reason (air) and emotion (water).

All Dick's planets are in the same or adjacent signs. Hence the only possible aspects between them are semi-sextiles or conjunctions. The same is partially true for Jenny except for the presence of the Leo Moon, introducing a jarring energy in the form of an opposition.

Now, let's sharpen our focus on the two individuals separately. Remember, it is vital when preparing compatibility assessments for two people, to analyse the two natal charts separately *before* comparing one to the other.

Some natal charts reveal that an individual will find it difficult to achieve a workable relationship with *any* partner, because his/her psychological make-up pulls against co-operation.

Other natal charts reveal individual needs clash violently with those of one possible partner but blend easily with those of another.

General Observations on Female Chart Patterns: Jenny

She likes a rather way-out lifestyle. A forward-looking, quite bohemian type who puts herself over with cool confidence. (Sun & Mercury in Aquarius. The mind backs up the ego. These are conjunctions).

Emotionally she's into dramatics, visibly passionate, expects adoration and aims to play it centre stage. (Moon in Leo contradicts Sun/Mercury behaviour. These are oppositions.) This contradiction is uncomfortable for her, confusing for her intimates.

In love/affection, Jenny's personality does yet another turnabout, making her tender, over-sensitive and wildly romantic. (Venus in Pisces: ego and mind don't know quite what to do with this sudden infusion of gushing sentimentality. These are semi-sextiles.)

In sexual responses, she repeats the fairy-tale syndrome. The bed partners of her dreams belong on the high road to Camelot and come complete with shining armour and white chargers. (Mars in Pisces: sexual fantasies [Mars] join up with affections [Venus] to create love scenes where reality never dares rear its ugly head. These are conjunctions.) Another hard one for ego/mind to handle. Most of the time, they camouflage it with Aquarian-style intellectualism.

Elemental Stress Patterns show very low earth score. No practicality, little basic commonsense. Intellectual whims of air, emotional drift of water and passionate rushes of fire govern — in that order.

Other Categories. Medium Cardinal score improves ability to thrust more purposefully for own objectives. Strong Fixeds score can, nevertheless, inject obdurate, unyielding attitudes. Low Mutable score suggests lack of quick adaptability to changes.

Now, let's look more closely at Dick.

General Observations on Male Chart Patterns: Dick

He, too is totally sold on the way-out lifestyle but it's a different style to Jenny's. He's a dreamy, many-coloured creature who puts himself over with shyness and sensitivity. Emotionally, he's just the same — only more so. (Sun and Moon in Pisces — the ego and emotions are swimming on the same wave. These are conjunctions.)

This blend, though comforting for him, is maddening to those who like their feet occasionally on solid ground. At times, he's so unworldly, he seems unreal.

Intellectually and in love, his personality performs a jolting turnabout, so that he appears impersonal, patronizing, disconcertingly detached. (Mercury and Venus in Aquarius — mind and affections team up to combat Pisces-style fantasizing. These are conjunctions.)

In sexual responses, he somersaults back into his previous deep-sea dreamworld. His ideal bed partner is also straight out of Camelot — the pining princess in the ivory tower (Mars in Pisces). This is a tough set-up for Aquarian mind/affections to work with. Struggling for air in the flood of sentimentality created by Piscean ego-sexuality, it promotes sudden, inconsistent changes in behaviour.

As with Jenny, Elemental Stress Patterns show low earth score, but slightly better than hers. Nevertheless, Dick is also far from being a practical planner. He is usually swept along by his emotional undercurrents, and at other times by intellectual flights of fancy. With very low fire score, he's lacking in energy and drive.

Other Categories. Low Cardinal score emphasizes Piscean tendency to float through life with little sense of purpose. Fair Fixeds score contains this meandering quality to some extent. Strong Mutable score implies change does not frighten. Equal Positive/Negative score adds better balance and prevents Piscean passivity from taking over the self.

From the foregoing individual planetary analyses, you can readily observe the existence of harmony and disharmony within Dick's own nature and Jenny's too. These will reflect themselves in the way both individuals handle any relationship — the current love affair or those which preceded or may follow it.

The Man-Woman Synthesis for Dick and Jenny (Rating table on p. 173)
Here, we begin by what I term 'Direct Cross-Referencing' of planets — i.e. Sun to Sun, Moon to Moon, etc.

Please be sure to note the following whenever you're comparing one partner's chart with the other's:

1.   The closer the 'orb' of aspect, the more intense the interaction of planetary energies, e.g. Partner A's Moon at 3 degrees of Leo will clash more forcefully with Partner B's Moon at 5 degrees of Aquarius than if the two Moons were farther apart by degree.

2.   If the orbs of aspect are very wide, do *not* discount the interaction of the two planets completely. Some astrologers recommend this course but I consider it very unwise.
      You are still faced with compatible or incompatible reactions between partners if, say, Partner A has Sun at 25 degrees of Gemini and Partner B has Sun at 10 degrees of Libra (similar life thrust). Or, say, where Partner A has Mercury at 6 degrees of Virgo and Partner B has Mercury at 19 degrees of Sagittarius (communication clashes).

3.   Semi-sextile aspects as discussed in Chapter 4 are important when cross-referencing charts. They can create irritating divergence in response.

4.   To provide an instant, *visual* spot-check when matching charts, rule *red* lines from the male partner's planets to the female's to mark clash points; rule *green* lines to mark comfortable contacts. But — in all cases, rule coloured lines *only* when the two planets concerned are within orb, i.e. within a maximum of 8 degrees of each other.

Dick and Jenny — Direct Planetary Cross-Referencing, Step by Step
First step: comparing the two Sun signs: (Pisces and Aquarius).
Indication = Blends or clashes in individual lifestyles, in the basic selves.

In this case, both partners are idealistic. But Dick is vague and unworldly. Jenny is much more rational though rather inflexible in opinions. Both sets of planets show a similar strong but uneasy blend of air (Aquarius) and water (Pisces) traits right through their personalities.

Further, air does not really enjoy the company of water — it feels saturated, damped down by such torrents of emotion. Water equally has a secret fear of air — it feels dried up, uncomfortably ruffled by the cold winds of reason.

Nevertheless, both Jenny and Dick are unusual, rather way-out types. Neither Aquarius nor Pisces are much concerned with convention or orthodox lifestyles. But Jenny's off-beat behaviour is of a far more obviously intellectual origin. Dick's stems from a highly emotional outlook.

Second step: comparing the two Moon signs: (Pisces and Leo). Indication = Blends or clashes in emotional response, in demonstrated feeling.

Not so good. Dick, though still tenderly sympathetic to all, behaves vaguely, too submissively in emotional encounters. Jenny's usual cool deserts her and she reacts passionately, theatrically. He feels consumed, evaporated by all that fire. She feels drowned, her fire quenched by the flood of fantasizing.

Third step: comparing the two Mercury signs: (Aquarius and Aquarius). Indication = Blends or clashes in methods of thinking, in intellectual communication.

On exactly the same beam here. Both Dick and Jenny think Aquarian-style — that is progressively, coolly, easily attracted to anything unorthodox in the way of ideas. It is, of course, easier for Jenny to think in this manner as her Sun backs it up heartily.

Dick's Sun does not do so. The way in which he talks and thinks fits less easily with the demands of his ego. Still, this link promises better sharing of ideas, more fruitful discussions.

Fourth step: comparing the two Venus signs (Aquarius and Pisces). Indication = Blends of clashes in affectional needs, in concepts of love.

Again vaguely unsettling. Dick is inflexible in his responses and dreads close ties with either a female or a family. Jenny's vision of love is almost childishly romantic, sensitive and impressionable. But she is not too keen on the daily round of home and babies, because neither belong in her fairy-tale love-nest.

Still, since these links repeat the Aquarius/Pisces emphasis notable throughout these two charts, some acceptance of each other's feelings is at least possible.

Fifth step: comparing the two Mars signs: (Pisces and Pisces)
Indication = Blends or clashes in sexual drives, in physical desires.

Spot-on once more. Under the eiderdown, both are equally gentle, equally impressionable and equally unrealistic. Except when Jenny's Leo Moon is on the prowl, genuine grand passion will never raise its fiery head but for this pair that's no loss. Both would be aghast if it did.

So much for direct planet-to-planet link-ups. Next, let's observe what happens when we apply diagonal cross-referencing to our test pair, i.e. Dick's Sun to Jenny's Moon, etc.

Dick and Jenny — Diagonal Cross-Referencing, Step by Step
Important Note. Again, when assessing compatibility, some astrological writers assert that unless the cross-referenced planets are within acceptable orbs, their influence should be ignored. As an astro-analyst, I disagree. Such an assertion can only be made if the psychological implications of planetary contacts are not understood.

The signs of each of the personal planets cannot help but attract or repel those of partner — regardless of orb — because each represents specific personality traits, which are themselves attractive or unattractive to the other individual. A turn-on or a turn-off.

Certainly if the orb between the two planets concerned is very wide, its effect on the relationship will be less forceful but still unquestionably in evidence.

However, to avoid filling up the rating table with possible confusing line detail, I have drawn in only those connecting lines between the planets of each partner which show in-orb aspects.

In Dick and Jenny's table, we observe there are only two in-orb *major* planetary link-ups when we cross-reference diagonally. These are a close conjunction between Dick's Mercury and Jenny's Sun, both in Aquarius (shown by green line) and a wide opposition between Dick's Mercury in Aquarius and Jenny's Moon in Leo (shown by red line).

The other four diagonal cross-references are all semi-sextiles.

Since semi-sextiles are far less formidable influences on compatibility, we'll list them very briefly below:

Dick's Pisces Sun   —   Jenny's Aquarius Mercury
Dick's Pisces Moon   —   Jenny's Aquarius Mercury
Dick's Pisces Mars   —   Jenny's Aquarius Sun
Dick's Aquarius Venus —   Jenny's Pisces Mars

Neither Aquarius nor Pisces are conventional in expectations of others or reactions. The sum total of above four aspects create a veering between intellectualized detachment and intermittent romanticism by both partners, but at different response levels. On occasions, this behaviour can promote a vague sense of unease, of not quite reaching each other.

Stronger Aspects

Dick's Pisces Sun — Jenny's Pisces Venus: This is a conjunction but well out of orb. His basic lifestyle of drifting along in pursuit of his latest dream appeals to her equally unrealistic affections. Fantasy ousts reality.

Dick's Pisces Moon — Jenny's Pisces Venus: An out-of-orb conjunction again. His fairy-tale world of emotion keeps her believing in happy-ever-afters.

Dick's Pisces Moon — Jenny's Pisces Mars: This is another conjunction but also well out of orb. Pretty much the mixture as before. In emotional/sexual encounters, both like to float on the tide of imaginings.

Dick's Aquarian Mercury — Jenny's Aquarian Sun: This is a conjunction and well within orb. His mentality sees itself reflected in Jenny's independent, unconventional way of life. He's interested in progressive ideas;; she lives them. It's a trip to the intellectual stratosphere for both.

Dick's Aquarian Mercury — Jenny's Leo Moon: This is an opposition but wider in its orb. A clear clash this time. Her demanding, commanding emotions dash themselves against his impersonal, super-cool thinking. She wishes he'd get down off his private Olympus. He wishes her mother had told her ladies don't go on like that.

Dick's Aquarian Venus — Jenny's Aquarian Sun: One more out-of-orb conjunction. Her good looks and inaccessible air add up to his vision of Super Woman. It has never occured to him that living with your imagined ideal instead of merely admiring it frequently add up to two very different kettles of fish.

Dick's Pisces Mars — Jenny's Pisces Venus: Again an out-of-orb conjunction. She's looking for a frog to turn into a prince and he's more than willing to play the part — in bed and out of it. Provided, of course, someone else buys the bed and pays the rent so he doesn't have to wear himself out working.

Man-Woman Synthesis for Dick and Jenny: The Verdict
No love relationship is totally idyllic or totally hellish. Dick and Jenny's is no exception. The attracting force here came from the constant emphasis on the signs of Pisces and Aquarius in both charts, creating a sense of similarity plus a powerful intellectual link and a fairly strong sex tie (the two Mercury and Mars conjunctions).

Jenny's Leo Moon is a possible source of trouble between them, although the opposition between it and Dick's Mercury can increase *initial* interest in each other. (Opposite attitudes attract first, irritate later.)

This pair may get to the altar but on the balance of probabilities, it's doubtful.

Dick is a triple-dyed Piscean (Sun, Moon, Mars), a true denizen of the deeps of his own fantasy world. A classic native of the Sign of the Fish. He dislikes ties and responsibilities and is capable of disappearing without so much as a ripple at the first hint of either. (As his first marriage proved!)

He knows this — deep down in the core of his being — and rightly suspects that Jenny's nature is too strong for his and could one day unman him. He may play the romance along right up to the last name on the wedding invitation list then vanish in the direction of cooler, calmer waters. Jenny would be wise to look for a stronger, more clearly defined personality in her partner, which six months later she did.

Of course, it is not the task of the analyst to supply the 'thumbs up' or 'thumbs down' verdict to any couple planning to marry. Their lives are their own. All you can do is point out the danger zones and the smooth sailing areas, then hand the final decision back to them. If both care enough about each other to overcome their differences and carefully circumnavigate potential conflict spots and personality clashes, the union will work. If they don't care enough, even the most ideally blended charts will bring their owners — sooner or later — to the point of no return.

Don't forget that in the case of Dick and Jenny, we worked only with

Solar Compatibility Rating. Had we analysed fully-erected charts (as we'll do later in this chapter), even more of this couple's pluses and minuses would have come to light. Nevertheless, we've learnt a lot from this technique so let's try it out one more time with two marriages that rocked the world.

Dick (27-2-1949)   **Jenny (29-1-1953)**

SOLAR COMPATIBILITY RATING TABLE

	His Personal Planets by Sign		Her Personal Planets by Sign
☉	8.00 ♓ (Ego)	☉	9.00 ♒ (Ego)
☽	4.00 ♓ (Emotions)	☽	3.00 ♌ (Emotions)
☿	11.00 ♒ (Mind)	☿	6.00 ♒ (Mind)
♀	26.00 ♒ (Affections)	♀	26.00 ♓ (Affections)
♂	12.00 ♓ (Sexuality)	♂	22.00 ♓ (Sexuality)

Note: As this book is not in colour, all *easy aspect lines* which are described in text as *green lines* in chart/table erection instructions are shown herein as *broken lines*.

All *challenging aspect lines* which are described in text as *red lines* are shown herein as *unbroken lines*.

	His Non-personal Planets by Sign		Her Non-personal Planets by Sign
♃	23.00 ♑	♃	11.00 ♅ R
♄	2.00 ♍ R	♄	27.00 ♎
♅	26.00 ♊ R	♅	15.00 ♋ R
♆	14.00 ♎ R	♆	23.00 ♎
♇	14.00 ♌ R	♇	22.00 ♌ R

His	Elemental Stress Patterns		Hers	
Fire	1	= 1	Fire 2 + ☽	= 3
Air	4	= 4	Air 4 + ☉	= 5
Earth	2	= 2	Earth 1	= 1
Water	3 + ☉ + ☽	= 5	Water 3	= 3

Planetary Categories		Planetary Categories	
Cardinal signs	2	Cardinal signs	3
Fixed signs	3	Fixed signs 5 + ☉ + ☽	
Mutable signs 5 + ☉ + ☽		Mutable signs	2
Positive signs	5	Positive signs 6 + ☉ + ☽	
Negative signs 5 + ☉ + ☽		Negative signs	4

The Love Goddess, the Baseball Hero and the Pulitzer Prize Winner

(The Marriages of Marilyn Monroe, Joe DiMaggio and Arthur Miller)

There's no better way of testing your theories in all areas of astro-analysis than to apply them to world-famous names. Why? Because the lives of such personalities are public property in the sense that just about every detail has been investigated, reported and recorded in books or encyclopaedias for posterity.

Tragic, mixed-up Geminian Marilyn Monroe has never been allowed to lie quietly in her grave since she died (allegedly by suicide) in August 1962. Even though decades have passed since then, her pictures still decorate poster shops and stories about her still pop up regularly in books, magazines and television shows. So if you don't know much about her comparatively short life to check our chart findings against documented events, you'll have no trouble hunting up the facts.

In my view, the best Marilyn biography is that written by eminent American intellectual Norman Mailer in 1973 and lavishly illustrated with photographs of Marilyn from infancy to just before her death as well as showing her in publicity shots with her two husbands — Joe DiMaggio and Arthur Miller.

Mailer's own interest in and penetrating comments on the world's sexiest siren spring from more than the fact that he and she were both born under air signs — as we'll see later.

Intriguing to note too that — although already a headliner herself — Marilyn clearly wasn't attracted to low-budget mediocrities for partners. Both her husbands share with her a biographical listing in *Encyclopaedia Britannica*, as do several of her rumoured lovers — fellow Geminian US President John Kennedy, Scorpion Robert Kennedy (his younger brother) and Sagittarian Frank Sinatra — to name only a few.

But, let's now take a mighty leap back in time to the 1950s and observe what astro-analysis could have told Marilyn if she had come for counselling prior to her marriages to Sagittarian Joe DiMaggio and Libran Arthur Miller.

In this section, on two separate rating table forms, you'll see listed the positions of the five personal planets for the respective birthdates of (1) Marilyn and Joe, and (2) Marilyn and Arthur. Be sure to follow the same rules we applied to the analyses for our ordinary test couple, Dick and Jenny.

Agreed, neither Marilyn nor her two husbands could be classed as ordinary people. Fame (and the tremendous ego drives required to attain it) made all three extraordinary, but V.I.P. status should never be allowed to blind the analyst to one paramount fact. Beneath the glamour and public image exist the same hopes and fears, the same search for love and happiness which motivates every human being, great or small.

Case No. 2: Marilyn Monroe, Joe DiMaggio, Arthur Miller
Subject data: *Marilyn Monroe* was born in Los Angeles, California on 1 June 1926 into a family of Irish extraction and named Norma Jean Baker. Biographies state she was abandoned by her father, reared partially in orphanages due to her mother's mental instability and pushed into an 'organized' marriage with the son of family friends at the age of 15 — to get her off everybody's hands. Her first bridegroom was a 19-year-old aircraft factory worker, named Jim Dougherty. Years later, he stated he thought he would be cradle-snatching the baby-faced, tomboyish, plumpish brunette. One date with Norma Jean convinced him otherwise. For a teenager of 1941, her sexual precocity staggered him.

By the time she met first Arthur Miller and then Joe DiMaggio, her life as bouncy, brown-haired little Norma Jean was far behind her. She had already become the blonde and busty Golden Girl of Hollywood.

Biographer Norman Mailer states she made a play for Arthur Miller some time before her introduction to DiMaggio but without success as he (Miller) was then still very much a married, family man.

Her much-publicized marriage to DiMaggio was of very short duration and she wed Miller in June 1956, although she never entirely broke her ties with either husband. Towards the end of her life, she turned first to one and then the other man, in between numerous affairs with actors and jet-setters. Shortly before her death a few weeks after her 36th birthday, she reportedly said Joe DiMaggio was her greatest friend.

Joe DiMaggio was born in Martinez, California on 25 November 1914 into a sizeable family of Italian background. Like Marilyn he rose to fame fast and by the age of 23 was well on the way to becoming a sporting legend. Biographers stated that he played baseball with such effortless expertise that ill-informed fans thought he was lazy. Two of his brothers were also top-name players.

When he was introduced to Marilyn he was nearing 40, had just retired from active sport and had already been married once. Considered a conservative and punctilious man, he was by then a household name for athletic brilliance.

More than twelve years older than Marilyn, he had reached the stage in life when his view of wedded bliss amounted to quiet evenings for two in front of the television set and nights out with his sporting cronies.

Biographer Norman Mailer describes their marriage as 'a war of egos, monumentally spoiled'. Yet for years upon years after her death, DiMaggio visited Marilyn's grave to lay red roses upon it.

Arthur Miller was born in New York City on 17 October 1915 into a middle-class Jewish family, graduating from the University of Michigan at the age of 23. Biographies describe him as a left-wing intellectual and a serious playwright, deeply concerned with morality and social pressures on ordinary people.

Not quite such an early winner as Marilyn and Joe, he hit the top in 1949 at the age of 34 when he won the coveted Pulitzer Prize for drama with his play *Death of a Salesman.* It was also rated the best play of that year and is still being staged nearly four decades after it was written.

Like Joe DiMaggio, Miller was considerably older than Marilyn — more than eleven years — and had known her some time before she encountered and married her baseball hero. Biographer Norman Mailer reports that later Marilyn 'chased Miller until he was caught' and received from him her third and last wedding ring inscribed: 'A to M, June 1956. Now is Forever'. In 1960, Miller wrote the novel for her last film, *The Misfits*, in which she also starred with her lifelong idol, Aquarian Clark Gable.

Marilyn was his second wife and at the time of her death, their marriage had broken up. Later Miller married a woman photographer.

Preliminary Observations on Man-Woman Synthesis:
Marilyn Monroe, Joe DiMaggio, Arthur Miller (Rating tables on p. 187)
We see merely from checking the ephemeris, the trio's personal planets are in these signs:

Marilyn

Sun	—	Gemini
Moon	—	Aquarius
Mercury	—	Gemini
Venus	—	Aries
Mars	—	Pisces

DiMaggio

Sun	—	Sagittarius
Moon	—	Pisces
Mercury	—	Scorpio
Venus	—	Sagittarius
Mars	—	Sagittarius

Miller

Sun	—	Libra
Moon	—	Aquarius
Mercury	—	Scorpio
Venus	—	Scorpio
Mars	—	Leo

So what conclusions can we draw about these marriages at first glance?

Again, the very simple exercise of completing the Solar Compatibility Rating Tables for Marilyn and her two husbands unearths some intriguing facts.

● Marilyn clearly preferred older men as marriage partners. This is, of course, a common psychological response in cases where a female child loses or is deserted by the father. It also explains in part her devotion to Clark Gable, born 1 February 1901. As a very young girl, she fantasized that he was her real father.

- Both DiMaggio and Miller were born less than a year apart and both with Mercury in Scorpio. This placement infers incisive, emotionally slanted thinking and very fixed ideas. Mentally then, neither man had much hope of communicating easily with Marilyn's own flitting, energy-scattering, irresponsible Mercury in Gemini.

- Not one of the trio had a solitary planet in earth. Thus plain, everyday common sense played little part in their life-planning. Air and water stresses dominate the chart patterns of Miller and Marilyn; fire and water do the same in DiMaggio's.

- All are thus overstresses on elemental patterns. Marilyn and Miller are caught between the demands of reason and emotions, thus both are capable of dashing off in pursuit of mental whims or emotional highs. Similarly, DiMaggio is tangled in a mesh of sudden passions and intense feelings, cares too much, reacts accordingly.

- All but one of the nine clash-points in comparing Marilyn's personal planets with DiMaggio's are oppositions, showing strong attraction coupled with underlying irritation.

- All but one of the four clash-points in comparing Marilyn's personal planets with Miller's are also oppositions, indicating a repetition of the same attraction/irritation response. However, with DiMaggio the opposing planets are all in mutable signs (Gemini/Sagittarius) whereas with Miller all are in cardinal signs (Aries/Libra) and thus harder to handle for both partners.

- Both Marilyn and Miller have the Moon in the same sign — Aquarius — thus backing up their air Suns, adding a sense of similarity, and creating a more cohesive personality impact. DiMaggio's Sun/Moon blend is contradictory (Sagittarius/Pisces) so in some ways he presents as a man divided against himself.

Now, let's examine the personalities of the three partners separately.

General Observations on Female Chart Patterns: Marilyn Monroe

She was into the flitting, flirting ever-changing lifestyle of the Twins personality type. Quick to change face, attitudes, ideas as the mood or fancy took her. Biographer Mailer observes she could switch from all-American angel to opportunistic computer in a flash. (Sun and Mercury in Gemini — here again the mind backs up the ego. These are conjunctions.)

Emotionally, she was detached, intellectualized feeling, oddly impersonal but with strong sense of superiority. (Moon in Aquarius — still in air element, so blends easily with Sun/Mercury behaviour. These are trines.)

Thus far it was all on a mental plane. Light, cool, whimsical, unthreatening. Play for fun but not for keeps.

In love/affection, Marilyn's personality suddenly heated up, making her unexpectedly ardent, eager, impetuous with little thought for anyone or anything but her own feelings. Biographer Mailer states that if Marilyn wanted a man, she chased him in no uncertain manner. (Venus in Aries — ego/emotions/mind are slightly nonplussed by this but as fire and air mix easily and with volatility, the show went on.)

In sexual responses, it was a dive off the deep end into fairy-tales, white knights, and happy ever afters. The tinsel-town fantasies of Hollywood love epics would all come true if she made them. (Mars in Pisces — a discordant water note in an air/fire sonata.)

This hidden vulnerability was disconcerting for both Marilyn and her intimates. It added to her screen appeal but depleted her vitality, confused her responses and beckoned to the half-world of dreams and drugs whenever reality ousted fantasy. Biographer Mailer states that she seemed 'bereft of social skin' and insomnia stalked her constantly. At first, she couldn't sleep when she failed to win applause in public or private life. Later, she couldn't sleep when she *did* win it.

Elemental Stress Patterns, as discussed earlier, show she shared with her two husbands a nil earth score. No practicality.

Other categories: Low Cardinal score exacerbated Geminian tendency to lack clear-cut goals but better determination came from strong Fixeds score. Good positive score developed added extroversion/assertion.

General Observations on Male Chart Patterns: Joe DiMaggio
He's into a restless, forcefully physical lifestyle with free-flowing, fiery

Sagittarian energy to fan the flames. Vigorous, vital, his well-attuned bodily co-ordination offered an almost inexhaustible reservoir of energy to achieve sporting brilliance. Plus the personal dignity and old-fashioned propriety, which biographer Mailer notes, were essential for great athletes of DiMaggio's era. (Sun, Venus and Mars all in Sagittarius. The ego, personal appeal and physical fireworks all team up to make a united front. These are conjunctions.)

Emotionally, the climate changes drastically. Back to the fairy story realm once again. A damp and dangerous infusion of softness/sentimentality which not only leaves him open to hurt but finds an echo, an answering response in Marilyn's undercover vulnerability. (This is a head-on clash for him, however.) Unsettling, depleting, the emotions feel themselves isolated among fiery living, fiery affection, fiery physical drives. (Moon in Pisces — Sun, Venus, Mars in Sagittarius. These are squares.)

Mentally, he's neither the 'hail-fellow-well-met' Centaur nor the impressionable Fish. He's wary, inclined to fixed opinions, allows his thinking to become emotionally slanted. Can be tough, sarcastic, intuitive, suspicious in the way he communicates. (Mercury in Scorpio — mind and emotions flow together but will often feel 'evaporated' by the fire planets. These are semi-sextiles.)

In love/affections/sexuality the fiery Centaur theme repeats itself again. Demonstrative, cheerful, not willing to be put into any kind of harness. (Venus/Mars in Sagittarius join in the hunt for freedom plus excitement. These are conjunctions.)

Although not really able to handle the Centaur responses, the Pisces Moon shares one need with them. An abiding dislike of permanent ties, continuing bonds.

Elemental Stress Patterns described earlier show DiMaggio shared with both wife and successor a nil earth score.

Other Categories. Low Cardinal score — same as Marilyn's — implies he hit his way to the top more through natural talent then unremitting effort. The zodiacal Centaur is remarkable for his unerring aim with an arrow. DiMaggio applied it to a baseball. Good Fixed score tends to hold down the Mutable tendency to change life direction too often and too easily. Fairly even Positive/Negative score shows he could give a bit and take a bit, never presenting as a steamroller type or a doormat.

General Observations on Male Chart Patterns: Arthur Miller

He's into the companionable, diplomatic, intelligentsia-oriented life of an up-market Scales Personality Type. That Libran middle-of-the-road approach fitted him perfectly 'to compose drama out of middle-class values' — to use biographer Mailer's phrase. Mailer also remarks Miller's success as a playwright was aided by the fact that 'he had dignity, looked the part, spoke in leftist simples that might conceivably be profound'. (Sun in Libra — only planet in the sign — but well supported by Moon in Aquarius. This is a trine.)

Emotionally, he's much the same as Marilyn. Secretly feels superior, retreats behind an intellectual wall, can't be easily moved by emotion. (Moon in Aquarius, mixing airily with the Sun in Libra infers no disturbing disharmony within the self.)

Mentally, there's a jolting breakaway from sophisticated intellectuality. Like predecessor DiMaggio, his thinking dives down into intuitive depths, can get into a groove, doesn't trust other people's statements or ideas. (Mercury in Scorpio — neither ego nor emotions are too comfortable with water-style mentality. These are out-of-orb aspects, a semi-sextile to Sun, a square to Moon.)

In love/affections, the water-style intensity stirs up brooding, secretive behaviour, possessiveness and easily-aroused jealousy. Soul-deep rapport is sought — the 'all or nothing at all' theme. (Venus in Scorpio lends a helping hand to the Scorpionic mentality. This is a very close conjunction.)

In sexual responses, there's a startling blaze-up of fire. Drives are commanding and demanding looking for mastery over intimates. Wants to be desired but prefers to be worshipped. (Mars in Leo — mind/affections stagger back from the heat — these are squares.)

Other categories. Medium Cardinal score. Higher than Marilyn's or DiMaggio's and boosted by the Sun. Better thrust and push. High Fixed score develops stronger gut faith in the self so Libran vacillation is checked. Very Low Mutable score implies fear of change, lack of adaptability. Fairly even Positive/Negative score with Positivity, strengthened by Moon/Sun points, increases extroversion.

Man-Woman Synthesis: Marilyn Monroe, Joe DiMaggio, Arthur Miller — Comparisons and Verdict

As we've already worked through direct and diagonal cross-referencing in compatibility analyses for our test couple, Dick and Jenny, we won't need to repeat the step-by-step method for Marilyn and her two husbands. Instead, we'll do it précis-style, focusing on major compatibility and clash-points.

Neither of Marilyn's marriages added up to plain sailing for any one of the participants.

1. *Marilyn and DiMaggio*

If we study the Solar Compatibility Rating Tables, we observe at once that DiMaggio's personal planets make no less than nine clash contacts with Marilyn's and pull all response levels into the conflict — ego, emotions, mind, affections, passions.

Sun links	DiMaggio's forcefully physical lifestyle collides with Marilyn's restless fluttering — with her flickering, changeable mind. (Sagittarius/Gemini oppositions.)
Moon links	DiMaggio's vulnerable, drifting emotional make-up is rebuffed by her flickering superficiality of mind and way of life. (Pisces/Gemini squares).

But a more comforting blend — his Moon to her Mars — promises better understanding of each other's needs at emotional/sexual level. (Pisces/Pisces conjunction.)

Mercury links	DiMaggio's stubborn, water-style mentality is chilled by her equally obdurate, airy, often eccentric emotional reactions. No meeting ground of minds/emotions. (Scorpio/Aquarius square).

But added rapport through talking over sexual needs and expectations — his Mercury to her Mars — offers hope. (Scorpio/Pisces trine.)

Venus links	DiMaggio's naturally physical expression of affection finds little continuing satisfaction from her 'let's-keep-

it-light' approach. (Sagittarius/Gemini oppositions again.)

But the two Venus', both in fire but well out-of-orb, suggest she could respond more passionately if and when the fancy took her. (Sagittarius/Aries trines — though with 22 degree orb.)

| *Mars links* | DiMaggio's energetic sexuality repeats the Venus clashes in his life with Marilyn. She adapts, reacts but often without real vitality. (Sagittarius/Gemini oppositions once again.) |

But a better blend — his Mars to her Moon — appears. She doesn't seek to fence him in (Sagittarius/Aquarius).

Added warmth also possible from his Mars and her Venus. Again both in fire but well out-of-orb. (Sagittarius/Aries trine — though with 18 degree orb).

| *Other plus or minus pointers* | Elements-wise, DiMaggio is obviously warmer, stronger, more vital but cannot detach himself as easily from life decisions as Marilyn. His emotionalism is more overtly displayed with Moon/Mercury in water. Hers is buried deep and dangerously for her air type personality, with only non-personal planets — Saturn, Uranus and Pluto — joining Mars in water signs. |

Both partners lack earthy practicality so neither would have considered the final outcome of their union and its spin-offs in other life sectors.

Both partners show similar determination/adaptability with similar Fixed/Mutable scores. Similar Positivity/Negativity scores also.

The Marilyn DiMaggio verdict: In another time, in another place, *and* if this pair had been ordinary people, the marriage could have worked.

Mutable sign types rarely attempt to dominate each other. Changeful, uncertain as to their own identity, they've got enough on their hands trying to run their own lives without running other people's as well. Further, mutable signs types usually respect the freedom of those close to them because they hate to be pinned down or trapped into routine themselves.

Yet, the fact that Marilyn's Venus makes no in-orb aspects with

DiMaggio's personal planets is somewhat ominous. It may not have mattered so much in an average couple's concern with each other. But Venus *is* the goddess of love and Hollywood packaged Marilyn as the love goddess of the Western world.

DiMaggio hated the trappings of sexual glamour the film bosses decreed for her — the plunging necklines, the skin-tight gowns, the wildly-publicized love affairs. Indeed, biographer Mailer reports that once married, DiMaggio expected his bride to forget about films and become a stay-at-home Italian-style housewife. That almost comic expectation is clearly consistent with the absence of Venus links in the cross-referenced charts of the couple.

Her public role as Venus incarnate was thus not integrated into their relationship and ignored by DiMaggio. Yet to Marilyn herself such a dethroning must have been like pretending most of her did not exist. Like casting in the dust that golden and glittering image which had transformed her from a penurious nonentity into the most famous female of the fifties.

Still, the overall view of the union suggests there was no real hurt for either partner in it, and that there was the basis for some genuine feeling. This was plainly evidenced by DiMaggio's undisguised grief at ex-wife's funeral. And all the years of the red roses for remembrance he brought to her grave.

In many ways Marilyn was right. DiMaggio *was* her best friend, sharing with her an oddly naïve (Piscean) simplicity that Miller would never begin to understand.

Passing on now to her third and last marriage, we switch the spotlight to the final act in the Marilyn story not long before the curtain began to fall.

2. *Marilyn and Miller*

This time our inspection of the Solar Compatibility Rating Table shows far fewer obvious trouble-spots but red lines alone are not the only yardstick we must judge by.

Intriguingly, *all* the tough cross-referenced aspects between Miller's personal planets and Marilyn's derive from her Aries Venus. Instantly we see this husband was far from turning his back on her Hollywood 'Venus' image. Instead he was ensnared, enthralled and deeply troubled by it. He instinctively felt it would help him retain his toehold on fame

— which it did. Those who are neither playgoers nor intellectuals know of Miller today, not as an outstanding dramatist but as Marilyn Monroe's last husband. Nevertheless, his first encounter with that Aries Venus of hers — impetuous, man-chasing, full-on and so oddly out of balance with her other personal planets — must have thrown his Libran Sun into a state of shock.

But Scales personalities love beauty, and when fully-armoured for battle with the camera, Marilyn had plenty of that. Plus it belonged to the type Libran males most savour. Soft, yielding, pink-and-white, sensually sweet. Non-threatening.

(Biographer Mailer mentions 'her sweet little rinky-dink of a voice' and goes on to say 'Marilyn suggested sex might be difficult and dangerous with others, but ice cream with her'.)

Sun links	Miller's somewhat stratospheric life style appeals to Marilyn's superiority-conscious emotional make-up. He presents as a high-minded intellectual — a role she also yearned to perform. Strange as that sounds, many biographers confirm it! (Libra/Aquarius trine).

But his stratospheric life style did not welcome her aggressive pursuit of affection. (Libra/Aries opposition).

Moon links	Miller's emotional needs are as detached and aloof as Marilyn's own. Emotions are regarded as ideas, not sensations (Aquarius/Aquarius conjunction). Further, they tune in easily to her light-minded Sun (Aquarius/Gemini trine).
Mercury links	Miller's Scorpio Mercury and Marilyn's Aries Venus are both close to the cusp of the adjacent sign: his to Libra; hers to Taurus. Hence beginners may not recognize this aspect as a 'hidden' opposition. Result? Not much chance of putting needs or disappointments into words.
Venus links	Again Miller's Scorpio Venus and Marilyn's Aries Venus show a similar cusp placement as in the preceding paragraph. Another 'hidden' opposition. Opposite and often irritating (to each other) manner of expressing love/affection.

Mars links   Miller's commanding sexuality appreciates Marilyn's versatility and many-faceted mind. She knows how to pick the right words to please (Leo/Gemini sextiles).

But another 'hidden' aspect — her Venus so close to Taurus — rocks the love boat through a square. His Leo Mars rightly concludes her sensuality is not solely concerned with him.

Other plus or   Elements-wise, Miller shows a similar score to Marilyn's.
minus pointers   No earthy practicality, little fiery spontaneity or overall ardour. Both attempt to satisfy the contrary demands of reason and emotion.

    Both partners have a fairly strong Fixed score so both are capable of determination in gaining their ends. Miller, though, is low on Mutables and Marilyn is high. He dislikes change, she loves it. Positivity/Negativity scores are similar.

The Marilyn/Miller Verdict: Not exactly an impossible mating but one more fraught with difficulties than comfort.

To begin with, although those born under the same element (in this case air) are often attracted to each other through a sensed similarity of interests, this self-same similarity can later breed familiarity and then boredom.

Next, Miller belongs to a cardinal sign and Marilyn to a mutable. In my experience, few mutable individuals can survive for long the resolutely one-pointed ego thrust of cardinal signs without submerging their identity and going under. 'Something's gotta give' as they say, and it's invariably the mutable person.

As biographer Mailer notes, Marilyn 'is ready to kill herself before she can allow his [Miller's] will to influence her will'. Finally, she fled.

Moreover, air type personalities are not truly supportive in times of trouble. That is not a criticism because propping up lost souls is not their job. Air looks mostly at the surface of things, prefers it to be bright and attractive and doesn't want to come close up to ugliness, despair or disharmony.

Miller and Marilyn were both cast in this mould. Yet when she began to fall apart, repeatedly attempting suicide, swallowing ever-stronger sleeping pills each night, fearful of ageing, unable to remember her lines when filming — the collapse was inexplicable to him. Biographer Mailer states Miller at this stage became 'a species of business manager, valet and in-residence hospital attendant'. A typical, logical, impersonal air-style method of dealing with illogical fears and nightmarish imaginings. It didn't work. It couldn't.

Miller, of his own nature, was far more concerned with 'the bleeding crowd' — as the rock musical 'Hair' put it — than 'with a needing friend'. Marilyn, at this last-ditch stage of her life surely needed a friend. She got a supervisor.

And so, this marriage went the way of Marilyn's earlier two towards the divorce court door. Helped on its downwards slide by the arrival in her life of one more lover (one more Libran too), French actor Yves Montand.

Incidentally biographer Mailer, born 31 January 1923, is an Aquarian with Mercury in the same sign. His air-type lifestyle and mentality would have undoubtedly helped to tune him into Marilyn during the writing of the big, 270-page biography published eleven years after her death — even more so because of her Aquarian Moon.

Joe DiMaggio (25-11-1914)   **Marilyn Monroe (1-6-26)**

SOLAR COMPATIBILITY RATING TABLE

	His Personal Planets by Sign		Her Personal Planets by Sign
☉	2.00 ♐ (Ego)	☉	10.00 ♊ (Ego)
☽	12.00 ♓ (Emotions)	☽	15.00 ♒ (Emotions)
☿	12.00 ♏ (Mind)	☿	6.00 ♊ (Mind)
♀	6.00 ♐ (Affections)	♀	28.00 ♈ (Affections)
♂	10.00 ♐ (Sexuality)	♂	20.00 ♓ (Sexuality)

His Non-personal Planets by Sign		Her Non-personal Planets by Sign	
♃	15.00 ♒	♃	26.00 ♒
♄	0.00 ♋ R	♄	21.00 ♏ R
♅	8.00 ♒	♅	28.00 ♓
♆	0.00 ♌ R	♆	22.00 ♌
♇	1.00 ♋ R	♇	13.00 ♋

Joe DiMaggio (25-11-1914)   **Marilyn Monroe (1-6-26)**

SOLAR COMPATIBILITY RATING TABLE

	His	Elemental Stress Patterns	Hers	
Fire	4 + ☉ = 5	Fire	2	= 2
Air	2 = 2	Air	4 + ☉ + ☽	= 6
Earth	0 = 0	Earth	0	= 0
Water	4 + ☽ = 5	Water	4	= 4

Planetary Categories		Planetary Categories	
Cardinal signs	2	Cardinal signs	2
Fixed signs	4	Fixed signs	4 + ☽
Mutable signs	4 + ☉ + ☽	Mutable signs	4 + ☉
Positive signs	6 + ☉	Positive signs	6 + ☉ + ☽
Negative signs	4 + ☽	Negative signs	4

Arthur Miller (17-10-1915)   **Marilyn Monroe (1-6-1926)**

SOLAR COMPATIBILITY RATING TABLE

	His Personal Planets by Sign		Her Personal Planets by Sign
☉	23.00 ♎ (Ego)	☉	10.00 ♓ (Ego)
☽	17.00 ♒ (Emotions)	☽	15.00 ♒ (Emotions)
☿	3.00 ♏ (Mind)	☿	6.00 ♓ (Mind)
♀	2.00 ♏ (Affections)	♀	28.00 ♈ (Affections)
♂	5.00 ♌ (Sexuality)	♂	20.00 ♓ (Sexuality)
	His Non-personal Planets by Sign		**Her Non-personal Planets by Sign**
♃	19.00 ♓	♃	26.00 ♒
♄	16.00 ♋	♄	21.00 ♏ **R**
♅	11.00 ♒ **R**	♅	28.00 ♓
♆	2.00 ♌	♆	22.00 ♌
♇	3.00 ♋ **R**	♇	13.00 ♋

	His	Elemental Stress Patterns	Hers	
Fire	2	= 2	Fire 2	= 2
Air	3 + ☉ + ☽	= 5	Air 4 + ☉ + ☽	= 6
Earth	0	= 0	Earth 0	= 0
Water	5	= 5	Water 4	= 4

Planetary Categories		Planetary Categories	
Cardinal signs	3 + ☉	Cardinal signs	2
Fixed signs	6 + ☽	Fixed signs	4 + ☽
Mutable signs	1	Mutable signs	4 + ☉
Positive signs	5 + ☉ + ☽	Positive signs	6 + ☉ + ☽
Negative signs	5	Negative signs	4

Much can be learned and applied to our own lives by telling sad stories of the death of love, warning us to watch for the first small crack in the foundations of marriage, teaching us how to learn now rather than pay later.

We've seen how significant chart patterns are triggered for better or worse by close contact with other human beings, and how these show up vividly even in Solar Compatibility Rating. Now, we're ready for the final step. In-Depth Compatibility Rating wherein the two fully-erected charts are blended together. This time our test couple are an actual pair of lovers we'll call Kurt and Rachelle.

To prevent identification and preserve confidentiality, their names and facts not relevant to the analyses have been changed. I have not stated their precise places of birth or their birth-times for the same reasons.

In this section, you'll find the two complete charts for this couple plus their Calculated Compatibility Rating Table. Here, we are also assessing appropriate house cusps and planetary house positions plus the Ascendants.

This example further illustrates the effect of mixing two different cultures, the situations which arise when one partner is already married and the effect of transplanting a love affair from one country to another.

We'll take short-cuts in description wherever practicable to avoid retracing the steps we've already studied in the preceding compability analyses.

In-Depth Compatibility Rating

Case No. 3 Kurt and Rachelle (Rating tables on p. 202)
Subject data

Kurt was born on 21 March, in Denmark. He is an industrial chemist, in his early forties, very successful and much travelled. He is married with four children but not happily. *Rachelle* was born on 9 April in

Australia. She is an academic in her mid thirties, has never been married, and has no children. The pair met on one of Kurt's lengthy business trips to Australia when he attended a professional dinner at which Rachelle was guest speaker. He moved in with her shortly after. It was decided she should come to Europe later while he made plans to divorce his wife.

Preliminary Observations on Man-Woman Synthesis: Kurt and Rachelle

We see from checking the individual charts, the couple's personal planets are in these signs and houses.

Kurt

Sun	Aries (Pisces cusp)	9th house
Moon	Capricorn	6th house
Mercury	Pisces	8th house
Venus	Pisces	9th house
Mars	Capricorn	6th house

Rachelle

Sun	Aries	9th/10th house cusp
Moon	Aries	9th house
Mercury	Aries (Pisces cusp)	9th house
Venus	Gemini	11th house
Mars	Leo	2nd house

So what can we pick up about this pair at first glance? As with Dick and Jenny, we see emphasis and cross-emphasis on the same signs, here Pisces and Aries, again indicating similarities of behaviour in ego thrust (Sun) and mentality (Mercury).

However, Kurt could be best described as a 'pretend' Aries with only the Sun in the sign and that by no more than 28 minutes. His Fire scores are not spectacular either, although boosted somewhat by the Ascendant and Midheaven.

Rachelle, on the other hand, is a 'three-star' Aries with three planets in the sign and a massive Fire score, stimulating mightily her natural Ram-type impatience, impetuosity and desire to live in the 'now' and forget about the 'afters'.

Obviously, then, Kurt is going to be far more cautious. Quite a pre-planner but his Pisces planets will allow him to be easily swept off his feet temporarily by romantic pyrotechnics. Not for long, of course, with Moon and Mars in canny, watch-your-step Capricorn. The Romeo and Juliet scene is one the Goat *never* plays for real!

At the time their love affair began, Kurt had just passed 40. As noted in Chapter 3, this is a dangerous, potentially self-deceptive age. Not only psychologically since it threatens the onset of middle age and diminished physical/sexual powers but also by virtue of a set of life-shaking planetary transits which start to hit everyone between 40 and 50 years.

It is a time when many males (and some females) consider discarding the existing life partner — who is usually near their own age and hence a reminder of ageing — for a younger mate.

Rachelle is seven years younger than Kurt. DiMaggio and Miller were both around 40 when they tangled with the much younger Marilyn Monroe.

Worth recording as well that it was Rachelle, not Kurt, who sought their compatibility analyses. The reason? His chart is easy for him to handle overall. I find that those with relatively simple charts rarely if ever ask for astro-analytical guidance. There is no unremitting conflict in their charts, so they feel little of it in their lives. Few doubts. Few nagging fears. Indeed, in the hundreds upon hundreds of charts I've worked through, I could count on my fingers the number of super-simple ones. And in every case, it was not the 'owner' of such a chart but the partner who sought guidance. But back to Kurt and Rachelle.

One danger signal which leaps out of both charts is the presence of two pairs of fantasy-generating Neptune oppositions — linking the 3rd and 9th houses in both cases. Kurt's Neptune opposes the Sun and Venus. Rachelle's Neptune opposes the Sun and Moon. Kurt's is a clash between mutable signs and thus not quite so hard to handle. Rachelle's is a clash between cardinal signs, adding force to the inner conflict.

The 3rd and 9th houses are not focal points as a rule in compatibility analyses so they have not been singled out for discussion earlier. In a book of this nature, it is necessary to presume some knowledge of the basics of astrological science on the part of readers. Therefore, if you don't easily follow the present comments, brush up by checking relevant sections of my companion book.

In the case of Kurt and Rachelle, the 3rd and 9th houses assume spot-on significance. Among other things, the 9th is the house of foreigners, long-distance journeys, potential culture clashes. The 3rd, among other things, is the house of communication, mental skills. Kurt is a Dane, Rachelle is an Australian. Both charts reveal their 'owners' are particularly sensitive to foreign influences. Kurt's Sun and Venus in the 9th will attract him to foreign-born men as friends/business associates, and to foreign-born women as lovers/partners. And he doesn't mind if they're somewhat forceful as Rachelle certainly is.

Rachelle's Sun is so close to the 10th house cusp, much of the energy would be diverted into the career scene but not all. Her 9th house Moon and Mercury firmly focus emotional and intellectual involvements on foreigners. (Kurt was neither the first nor the last European she was attracted to.) He is a highly educated man, which suits her Mercury. With some capacity for romance in love affairs which suits her Mars.

Sadly, though, tough Neptune aspects promise little joy in the long-run for a love affair as it swiftly drifts into the Neptunian dream world. And, when the current changes, drifts away into a fog of delusions, fantasies and false hopes.

Perhaps, you're thinking now: 'Not another disaster? Aren't we ever going to have one with a happy ending?' No, not here. Certainly, I have on file plenty of stories of troubled unions which changed into happy ones — because the participants both got the message from their charts and tried harder. Couples who started out on the right foot instinctively choosing the right mate, never appear in my files because such marriages never need counselling or guidance. Remember too, the purpose of this book is to demonstrate how to learn from the mistakes of others so you won't fall into the same chasms of misunderstanding yourself.

Whenever I counsel couples on compatibility, I first dictate two separate 60-minutes tapes of individual chart analysis, using the techniques set out in *How to Astro-Analyse Yourself and Others*.

If you plan to act as advisor to yourselves, friends or family, I strongly recommend you follow a similar course so that you thoroughly understand the personality you're considering as a single person as well as a member of a pair.

Quick-Reference Forms — Natal Personality Profile plus Compatibility Rating Profile

In the following pages, you'll find profiles (a psychological term for the summary of individual charactertistics) on our present test couple — Kurt and Rachelle. With them are a set of blank forms (see p. 213). Copy or photocopy the forms for your own analyses.

I have personally designed these simplified profiles to offer a Visual Learning Programme that will set the analytical procedures firmly in your mind and keep you thinking according to the principles of scientific method. They will also allow you to examine the subject's personality in graphic outline — rather like a blueprint — and therefore ensure you pick up its salient features at a glance.

As you'll have guessed by now, I have no patience with those who hold astrology out as some form of clairvoyance, soothsaying or a branch of the occult arts. In my view, it is plainly a science and should be treated and taught on a solidly scientific basis. To take it any other way leads to confusion, fortune-teller-style rambling and error.

Clip your completed profiles into a ring file alongside your own chart work for instant reference whenever required. This practice will also help you check your own progress as an analyst.

But Profiles are for your eyes only. Do not give them out to those you are advising. Comments therein are necessarily brief, blunt and couched in technical terms.

When discussing compatibility pointers with subjects, take care to rephrase your statements as tactfully and positively as possible. Put them in layman's terms also to ensure they can be thoroughly and easily understood.

I'm not suggesting, of course, that you gloss over trouble spots and personality defects on the one hand. Or that you pronounce dire verdicts on the other.

In my view, both above are common failings among practitioners who have no psychological training. Clients have shown me analyses so ludicrously sugary they almost stick to your fingers, or so heavily negative, their subjects are as good as told to sign a suicide pact and get it over with!

Honesty, tactfully and realistically phrased, is always the best policy. Again, if you don't perceive quickly why specific comments are set down on our sample profiles, reread appropriate chapters in this or its companion book. A good encyclopaedia of astrological terminology is also a worthwhile and inexpensive investment.

Summary of Natal Chart Indicators: Analyst's Report — Rachelle

1. *HEMISPHERE EMPHASIS:* 5 planets above horison; 5 below horizon

   Thus something of Universal Woman type. Career drives strong but will never be pursued at expense of private satisfaction.

8 Cardinal signs	4 + ⊙ + ☽ + Asc + MC	
3 Fixed signs	3	
3 Mutable signs	3	
13 Positive signs	10 + ⊙ + ☽ + MC	
1 Negative sign	0 + Asc	

10 Fire signs	7 + ⊙ + ☽ + MC	
3 Air signs	3	
0 Earth Signs	0	
1 Water sign	0 + Asc	

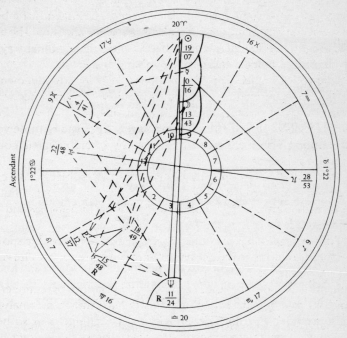

Name Rachelle

B.T.Q.	Planet	Natal	Aspects
P C A	3 ♆ Neptune	11.24 ♎ R	* ♇
P M A	12 ♅ Uranus	22.48 ♓	
P F F	2 ♄ Saturn	15.48 ♌ R	♂ ♇ * ♆
P M F	6 ♃ Jupiter	28.53 ♐	☍ ♅
P F F	2 ♂ Mars	18.49 ♌	♂ ♇ ♂ ♄ * ♅
P C F	10 ⊙ Sun	19.07 ♈	♂ ☽ Δ ♇ Δ ⚹ * ♅ ☍ ♆ Δ ♄
P M A	11 ♀ Venus	4.41 ♓	Δ ♆
P C F	9 ☿ Mercury	0.16 ♈	* ⚹ □ ♃
P C F	9 ☽ Moon	13.43 ♈	Δ ♇ Δ ☍ Δ ♄ ☍ ♆
P F F	2 ♇ Pluto	12.37 ♌ R	

2. *POSITIVITY/NEGATIVITY EMPHASIS:* 13 points positive; 1 point negative

   Massive overstress. Likely to find it virtually impossible to take orders or accept any form of male domination. Far too assertive in most life situations. Exacerbates Ram-type pushiness. Must try to learn to put other's needs before own.

3. *REACTIONAL MODE EMPHASIS:* 8 points Cardinals; 3 points Fixeds; 3 points Mutables

   Slightly better balance here but again one-pointed drive for own objectives/goals dominates. Fair determination. Fair adaptability.

4. *ELEMENTAL EMPHASIS:* 10 points fire; 3 points air; 0 points Earth; 1 point Water

   Massive overstress again. Much too fast, reckless, impulsive. Some capacity to detach and think way out of problems. No real practicality at all. Does not understand own emotions.

5. *ANGULAR PLANETS STRESS:* 1 Angle only stressed — Sun on 10th cusp.

   Career again brought into sharper focus. Wants fame and honours. Self-expression (1st); home affairs (4th); relationships (7th) all empty houses. Lessened gut concern with these life sectors.

6. *NOTABLE CONFIGURATIONS:* Small stellium in 2nd — Mars, Saturn, Pluto

   Energy, self-discipline and penetrating perception all focused on financial matters. Goes after money. Should succeed income-wise if controls headstrong tendencies.

7. *POWER POINT CHARACTER PATTERN:*
   Ascendant — Cancer (Gemini Cusp)
   Sun   — Aries
   Moon   — Aries

   Ram personality traits heavily stressed. Some clash possible with less extroverted traits of Crab Ascendant. More rashly aggressive than may seem at first encounter.

8. *LOVE AND SEX NATURE:*
   Moon Sign: Aries   Moon house: 9th
   Venus Sign: Gemini   Venus house: 11th
   Mars Sign: Leo   Mars House: 2nd

   Fire/Air Mix. Very volatile. Emotions flare up quickly, foreign-born types appeal. Affections communicative but changeable. Large following of friends/acquaintances likely. Sexually very temperamental and commanding. But physical energies are directed towards earning money — away from private affairs.
   Moon/Mars signs infer attraction to fire-type males.

9. SUCCESS DRIVES:
   Mercury: Aries (Pisces Cusp): House: 9th
   Jupiter: Sagittarius: House: 6th
   Saturn: Leo: House: 2nd

   Again, a volatile Fire/Air Mix. Usually impulsive, quickly-reactive thinker but may at times be influenced by others — especially foreigners. Optimistic about opportunities for betterment which are likely through work 'lucky breaks'. Ambitions dramatically conceived, a high-flyer but needs to apply self.

10. *MAJOR PLANETARY ASPECTS:*
    Sun: 5 helpful; 1 difficult

    Should benefit from: better sense of togetherness; added leadership qualities and vitality; inventive approach; improved ability to eradicate faults in self.

    Needs to watch: impracticality, escapism, deception from self or others — especially males. Can be gullible.

    Moon: 3 helpful; 1 difficult

    Should benefit from: vigorous, warm, enterprising approach in liaisons; added supportiveness and responsibility towards intimates; improved capacity to perceive own motivations and those emotionally close.
    Needs to watch: self-delusive tendencies, escapism yet again, deception by females.

    Mercury: 1 helpful; 1 difficult

Should benefit from: added charm and ease in putting over ideas/opinions.

Needs to watch: over-enthusiasm, faulty judgment, careless trusting to luck in mental pursuits.

Venus: 1 helpful

Should benefit from: added sensitivity and pleasant form of sentimentality in love/friendship.

Mars: 1 helpful; 2 difficult

Should benefit from: improved capacity to respect freedom of others, added personal charisma.

Needs to watch: explosive reactions, waste of energies, inhibited, rejecting beheviour.

Personality Profile and Summary of Natal Chart Indicators — Kurt

1. *HEMISPHERE EMPHASIS:* 7 planets above horison, 3 below horizon

   Generally more concerned with career and the professional scene than with private life. Success-oriented type.

2. *POSITIVITY/NEGATIVITY EMPHASIS:* 5 points Positive; 9 Negative

   Presents problems. Not easy to express or assert the self. With strong pressure/opposition from more positive personalities, likely to become passive and self-suppressive.

3. *REACTIONAL MODE EMPHASIS:* 6 points Cardinals; 5 points Fixeds; 3 points Mutables

   Fairly good balance here. Sufficient personal drive and gut confidence to combat underlying passivity some of the time but not all. Mutable score allows better ability to handle new situations, alien cultures.

4. *ELEMENTAL EMPHASIS:* 5 points Fire; 0 points Air; 7 points Earth; 2 points Water

   Contrary mix. Earth plays the dominant role, forcing a more

6	Cardinal signs	$3 + \odot + \mathbb{D} + MC$
5	Fixed signs	$4 + Asc$
3	Mutable signs	3
5	Positive signs	$2 + \odot + Asc + MC$
9	Negative signs	$8 + \mathbb{D}$

5	Fire signs	$2 + \odot + Asc + MC$
0	Air signs	0
7	Earth Signs	$6 + \mathbb{D}$
2	Water signs	2

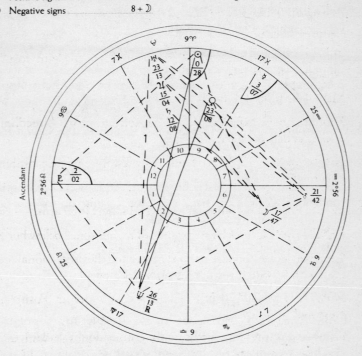

Name Kurt

B.T.Q.	Planet	Natal	Aspects
N F E	3 ♆ Neptune	26.13 ♍ R	＊ ♇
N F E	10 ♅ Uranus	23.13 ♉	△ ♆
N F E	10 ♄ Saturn	12.08 ♉	
N F E	10 ♃ Jupiter	15.04 ♉	♂ ♄ ♂ ♅
N C E	6 ♂ Mars	21.42 ♉	△ ♃ △ ♅ △ ♆
P C F	9 ☉ Sun	0.28 ♈	△ ♇ ♂ ♀ ☍ ♆
N M W	9 ♀ Venus	23.08 ♓	＊ ↗ ＊ ♅ ☍ ♆
N M W	8 ☿ Mercury	3.07 ♓	⊼ ♇
N C E	6 ☽ Moon	17.47 ♉	＊ ↗ ♂ ↗ △ ♃ △ ♄ △ ♅
P F F	1 ♇ Pluto	2.02 ♌	

practical, look-before-leaping attitude. Can be impulsive but only briefly. Without Air, easily becomes enmeshed in own worries and fears. Strong sense of duty/responsibility.

5. *ANGULAR PLANETS STRESS:* 2 Angles stressed; Pluto on 1st cusp; Jupiter, Saturn, Uranus in 10th.

Strong desire for personal freedom — somewhat of a 'a law unto himself.' May appear biddable but isn't. Professional life successes paramount. Grasps opportunities, works resolutely, applies originality but acts as own master in job scene at all times.

6. *NOTABLE CONFIGURATIONS:* Small Stellium in 10th. Grand Trine in Earth — Mars Uranus, Neptune.

Easy successes in life sectors linked in the trine; i.e. working environment, professional achievement, acquisition of appropriate educational skills. Cuts back on drive if gains too easily made. Attainment again stressed.

7. *POWER POINT CHARACTER PATTERN:*
Ascendant = Leo
Sun   = Aries (Pisces cusp)
Moon   = Capricorn

Lion, Ram, Fish and Goat traits struggle for supremacy. Commanding presence likely, masking inner doubts and wavering, plus heavy emphasis on status and security.

8. *LOVE AND SEX NATURE:*
Moon sign = Capricorn   Moon house = 6th
Venus sign = Pisces   Venus house = 9th
Mars sign = Capricorn   Mars house = 6th

Earth/water mix — strong but fluid — Emotions and energies concentrate on work effort. Very unrealistic, vulnerable in love/friendships with foreign-born individuals. Likely to trust and doubt others — at the same time. All three planets direct their influence away from private relationships. Not really a 'personal' man.

Moon/Venus signs infer attraction to Earth/Water type females.

9. *SUCCESS DRIVES:*

Mercury sign	= Pisces	Mercury house	= 8th
Jupiter sign	= Taurus	Jupiter house	= 10th
Saturn sign	= Taurus	Saturn house	= 10th

Again, an Earth/Water mix. Often inspired, intuitive thinker — vivid imagination. Works with money of others. Attracts attention of influential figures professionally. Opportunities and ambitions pursued steadfastly with strong desire for material gain.

10. *MAJOR PLANETARY ASPECTS:*
Sun: 2 helpful; 1 difficult

Should benefit from: added capacity to use charm, appear cultured; improved ability to eradicate faults in self — not unpleasantly egotistical.

Needs to watch: Impracticality, escapism, deception from self or others — especially males. Can be gullible.

Moon: 4 helpful; 1 problematical

Should benefit from: more sensitive expression of emotions; added optimism and generosity, beneficial emotional contacts — further supportiveness, dutiful to intimates — does not crowd others, inventive in emotional behaviour.

Needs to watch: emotional irritability, over-reactions, misdirected push.

Mercury: No major aspects.

Venus: 2 helpful; 1 difficult

Should benefit from: warmer display of affection/friendship; better sense of timing in relationships.

Mars: 3 helpful; 0 difficult

Should benefit from: more responsive, less inhibited responses; added magnetism and respect for freedom of intimates; increased intuitive understanding of sexual partner.

Male Partner: Kurt   **Female Partner: Rachelle**

CALCULATED COMPATIBILITY RATING TABLE

	His Personal Planets by Sign and Degree		Her Personal Planets by Sign and Degree
☉	0.28 ♈ (Ego)	☉	19.07 ♈ (Ego)
☽	17.47 ♑ (Emotions)	☽	13.43 ♈ (Emotions)
☿	3.07 ♓ (Mind)	☿	0.16 ♈ (Mind)
♀	23.08 ♓ (Affections)	♀	4.14 ♓ (Affections)
♂	21.42 ♑ (Sexuality)	♂	18.49 ♌ (Sexuality)

1. *CHILDHOOD CONDITIONING:*
   Male Partner: sign on 4th: Libra
                 Planets in 4th: Nil
   Female partner.: sign on 4th: Libra
                    Planets in 4th: Nil

Remarks (male):

Air-type parents likely; conditioned to seek home scene where easy exchange of ideas and continuing mental stimulation offered; strong desire for harmony and agreeable types with which to share home; not deeply concerned with domesticity — no planets to focus life on home matters.

Remarks (female):

Same pattern: same comment.

2. *MARITAL/PARTNERSHIP EXPECTATIONS*
Male partner: sign on 7th: Aquarius
Planets in 7th: Nil
Female partner: sign on 7th: Capricorn
Planets in 7th: Nil

Remarks (male):

Instinctive search for air-style living repeats; seeks open unions, unusual women; wants well-educated, communicative mates; absence of planetary focus here implies life force not focused on long-term involvements.

Remarks (female):

Instinctive search for earth-style partnerships; seeks steady, successful personalities with proven status; wants strong, practical men; can be manipulative, dogged in gaining desires; absence of planetary focus here same as current partner.

3. *ROMANTIC IDEALS — CONCERN WITH CHILDREN:*
Male partner: sign on 5th: Sagittarius
Planets in 5th: Nil
Female partner: sign on 5th: Scorpio
Planets in 5th: Nil

Remarks (male):

With the casual, easy-come-easy-go sign of Sagittarius on the 5th, love affairs usually initiated and ended more quickly and with less lasting concern; interest in children somewhat sporadic; not likely to act the authoritative parent; absence of planetary focus here implies does not need to express through offspring or load own ambitions on to them.

Remarks (female):

With the intense, all-or-nothing sign of Scorpio on the 5th, love affairs built up into emotional storms; dominating, demanding, behaviour likely; interest in children not stressed but could be possessive, highly directive towards them; absence of planetary focus same here as current partner.

4. SOCIAL PROJECTION/COMMUNICATION

Male partner: Ascendant: Leo
Mercury: Pisces
Female partner: Ascendant: Cancer (Gemini Cusp)
Mercury: Aries (Pisces Cusp)

Remarks (male):

Projects as vigorous, lordly individual, impact somewhat softened by proximity to rather timorous Cancer cusp; appears confident at first contact.

Intuitive communicator; picks up on social 'vibes' quickly; may seem wandering, vague in discussion.

Remarks (female):

Projects as sensitive, caring individual; impact fragmented by proximity to more talkative Gemini cusp; appears on guard at first contact.

Diverse communicator; forceful, thrusting mostly but may drift into rambling talk. Fairly unpredictable in discussion.

5. CATEGORY COMPARISONS

Male partner: Elements: Earth/Fire stress
Polarities: Negative stress
Modes: Cardinal/Fixed stress
Female partner: Elements: Fire/Air stress
Polarities: Positive stress
Modes: Cardinal stress

Remarks:

She inclines to leading, expects him to follow. She is impulsive at several response levels; he is less spontaneous, more prudent. He will accept direction to some extent: she will not endure it in any form. He needs to assert, she to reduce demand.

6. PLANETARY CROSS-REFERENCING (Shown in Graphic Form on Rating Table)

Direct

Remarks:

Male Sun to Female Sun: out-of-orb conjunction. Promotes sense of similar life goals but can cause some friction, lack of stimulation.

Male Moon to Female Moon: in-orb square. Promotes diverse and conflicting emotional behaviour, creative of misunderstandings, disappointments.

Male Mercury to Female Mercury: slightly out-of-orb semi-sextile. Promotes vague sense of unease in communication.

Male Venus to Female Venus: out-of-orb square. Promotes differences in affectional behaviour and type of pleasures enjoyed.

Male Mars to Female Mars: out-of-orb inconjunct. Promotes divergent, overly subjective reactions in sexual/physical activities.

Diagonal

Remarks:

(a) *Compatible aspects:*

Male Sun to Female Mercury. Exact conjunction. Promotes more comfortable blend of lifestyles and mentality, boosting agreement on important issues.

Male Sun to Female Venus: in-orb sextile. Promotes greater attraction and fondness, creative of better co-operation and understanding of romantic ideals.

Male Venus to Female Mercury: wide-orb, hidden conjunction. Promotes better blending of shared social, cultural and intellectual interests, boosting common enjoyment of leisure.

(b) *Incompatible aspects:*

Male Moon to Female Sun: in-orb square. Promotes diminished ability to identify with contrary responses in personal styles and emotional responses.

Male Mercury to Female Venus: in-orb square. Promotes irritations and communication breakdowns, creative of clashes between differing manners of thinking and feeling.

Male Mars to Female Sun: in-orb square. Promotes anger, quarrelling and overbearing behaviour, creative of continuing dissent on intimate matters.

Male Mars to Female Moon: wide-orb square. Promotes hyper-sensitivity, inhibited responses, dissatisfaction in lovemaking through contrary expectations.

Summary of findings from Chart Comparisons

As per 1: Similar early life experiences likely: both partners intelligent and harmony-seeking in home scene. A helpful indicator.

As per 2: Differing needs but each can deliver — to reasonable extent — expectations of other. Not a seriously damaging indicator.

As per 3: Possible risk area. Romantically, he's more of a player, she's out for total conquest. Problematical indicator.

As per 4: Social mask camouflages basic selves in both partners. He is less organizing than he appears. She is more so. Both capable of meandering, water-style communication. Possible balancing factor but should not rush into commitment. Much longer acquaintance needed.

As per 5: Another risk area. He may feel he is being 'taken over'. In time, can cause resentment on his part. She may mistake his desire to be agreeable for weakness.

As per 6: More difficult links than easy ones. Her forcefulness can lead to sexual problems. He is capable of exhibiting some of the fiery, passionate behaviour her Moon/Mars signs demand, but only at superficial levels. She has little of the practical supportiveness and emotional softness his Moon/Venus signs demand. Shared intellectual and leisure interests assist relationship.

As you can see, the profiles and rating tables provide a quick-reference, permanent record of complete analyses. They will also help to teach you to apply scientific method to your thinking, so that you never overlook vital points in analysis, or overemphasize certain traits at the expense of others or ramble off into meandering comments.

The Kurt/Rachelle Verdict

On a scale of 1 to 10, this union would only be awarded a score of 5. As with all relationships, there are pluses and minuses, points of agreement, points of dissent.

Kurt's fortyish age grouping, the facts that he was already married with a family but more than 13,000 miles from home and alone in a foreign country — all added up to warning lights that Rachelle would have been wise to consider.

Had she paused long enough to know him better through his chart as well as her own observations, she would have seen he might play the affair Pisces-style, furnishing their castles in the clouds with romantic fantasies and rose-tinted daydreams which could disappear in the proverbial puff of smoke when it was time come back to earth.

His chart patterns do not suggest there was any conscious attempt to deceive Rachelle as to his intentions. At the time they met he was undoubtedly attracted — probably more by her Ascendant manner and her intelligence (Mercury link). He was feeling slightly lost in a new city and she offered him a welcome anchor.

His part-Pisces Sun and Pisces Venus would have encouraged him to float into what looked like a pleasant liaison. His Leo Ascendant would have happily responded to her full-on attentions and undisguised admiration. His Moon and Mars, both in Capricorn, would not have hesitated to make use of what opportunities presented themselves.

Always impulsive, imprudent and inclined by her chart to rush in where angels feared to tread, Rachelle was convinced she had at last found the man of her dreams and was in anything but a wait-and-see mood.

The love affair flourished during the eight weeks he lived with her in Australia. Later that year, although he had written only two friendly letters, she resigned from her job and followed him to Europe.

When she landed, he welcomed her in a courteous but disconcertingly formal manner. Back in his own country, he seemed a different man. He invited Rachelle at once to his home to meet his children and housekeeper, explaining his wife was away on a visit to her parents. Over afternoon tea, he mentioned that she (Rachelle) was a valued business associate from Australia.

No matter how hard she tried, he would not discuss their relationship or the plans she thought they had made. She stayed a couple of weeks without managing to make contact with him again and then returned home, hurt and bewildered.

The last scene was heavily Neptunian, directed by the awkward 9th house Neptune oppositions in both their natal charts. She had rushed off in pursuit of a foreign-world fantasy; he had evaded a confrontation by pretending there was nothing to confront.

In many ways, this is not an uncommon story which can happen to anyone when love, passion, loneliness or any other intense feeling make us forget the differences between the 'then' and the 'now'. Like many others in similar circumstances, Kurt had not meant to deceive Rachelle. The scene had simply changed and so had he.

If Rachelle had heeded the warnings the charts gave, she could have saved herself from a very painful experience, costly not only in emotional hurt but also in money and job security. (The latter problems are often disregarded in the heat of a passion but can hit like bricks later.)

I knew she would not listen to anything smacking of caution. Strongly fire types rarely do — that's part of their appeal — and once they dash off in pursuit of a dream, they seldom turn back. I could only hope that when the disorienting outcome arrived, she was better able to accept it and to learn from it.

In any event, had Kurt kept his promises I doubt that a long-term relationship would have worked satisfactorily for either partner. The links were not powerful enough to hold fast against such mundane problems as her possible inability to work in his country or vice versa, the divorce and its unavoidable emotional and financial strains, and the differing cultural backgrounds.

It was, of course, far easier for me as a third party to look at their relationship by means of their charts dispassionately and impartially. To see what Rachelle could not see — or didn't want to. The vital difference here was that I was outside the affair and she was in it. That is the advantage the analyst always has although it is one that must be gently exercised. Otherwise, you cast yourself in the role of that awful character — a know-all, 'told-you-so' spoilsport.

Living, Learning and Loving Again

The Kurt-Rachelle story (like the others previously discussed) is visible evidence of how astro-analysis can minimize the margins of error in relationships. Of how the heightened awareness of our own motivations and those important to us that the charts proffer can help avoid dangerous situations or at least recognize them as such.

Agreed, we cannot reduce the process of finding the perfect partner to a cold-blooded chart computation of each candidate's personality assets or liabilities. We can, nevertheless, use the charts to prevent us from 'flying blind' into a pairing that may or may not be workable — in terms of our own hopes, expectations and conditioning.

Not that I believe for one moment that any analyst should regard himself/herself as some sort of omnipotent mastermind, directing lives from above, or that those who seek advice should be allowed to gain such an impression.

Carl Gustav Jung, the great psychoanalyst, was born under the commanding sign of Leo but always said that no counsellor should play God. The counsellor's role is chiefly to point out personality traits, good or bad, and indicate from studying them the consequences of a particular course of action.

Albert Einstein, the great physicist, was born under the visionary sign of Pisces but once remarked: 'I do what my nature drives me to do.' So do you. So do I.

Therefore the decision to act or not to act at a specific time in a specific manner *must* always remain the individual's own. Even the chart itself does not allow us to step inside another person's mind and spirit or assume control of his/her life. Those who attempt to do so — through the astrological chart or any other means — are presumptuously taking away the free will that is the prerogative of every human being. We are not our brothers' keepers. We are not in their shoes.

Many are the times that clients have sought to push me into this role of godlike arbiter of their fates with questions like: 'When will he marry me' . . . 'I've been told I'm going to marry a tall, fair man. When will I meet him?' . . . 'Will my ex-wife come back to me?' . . . 'Will I marry into money?'

You'll observe the constant stress on the world 'will'. And, if you read between the lines of such questions, you'll deduce a perhaps unrecognized expectation that all the hoped-for events will come about without the questioners making the slightest effort to attain their goals. Rather like miraculous bolts from the blue. And merely because somebody else says so.

I always refuse those 'Will' questions, pointing out that astro-analysis, unlike fortune-telling astrology, does not claim to give 'Yes' or 'No' answers. Instead it shows us how to work effectively within the structure of our own personalities to achieve what is right for us rather than just lying back and waiting for prophesied love dreams to come true, or prophesied love disasters to drop us in our tracks.

So don't be cajoled when advising others into the 'Will' or 'Won't' business. It is a dangerous practice for the counsellor — misleading to the counselled. Some mistakes in relationships and all other major life choices *have* to happen to teach us who we are and what we can or cannot do. They are an integral part of the living and learning process.

I know I've made plenty of mistakes in my own life but far fewer since I understood the charts of those close to me. Understanding brings tolerance of the faults of others and reminds you constantly of your own.

Very often unhappy love affairs or broken marriages allow you to see yourself in a new light, forcing needed personality changes that will bring better luck next time.

Learning from the past — instead of regretting it *or* living in it — is the real secret of happier ever afters! Or if things have gone wrong for you once or twice, don't let yourself fall into the 'I'll never let myself be hurt like that again' trap. I know what it feels like. It very nearly happened to me after my first husband died suddenly when he was 24 and I was 22. I still remember only too well the initial shock, the terrible emptiness, the heart-breaking task of going through piles of condolences, the effort required to pick up the pieces of your life and start putting them back together again. But the pieces can and must be picked up. What's more people will soon lose patience with you if you spend your time bemoaning your unhappy fate, or extolling the virtues of a lost love at the expense of a new-found one.

The at times devious processes of memory can lead us away from the realities of a past relationship. As years pass, distance lends enchantment to the view. Faults are forgotten. Good times erase the bad. A human being gradually becomes idealized into superhuman perfection. This trick of memory should be consciously controlled or you will never find happiness again. It is unhealthy for you to live in the past and damaging to your relationships with all around you.

Certainly, there's no denying you can spare yourself a lot of pain if, after one sad or bad experience, you resolutely turn your back on love. The problem is you'll be turning your back on living as well. Shutting the door on life. So should a relationship end unhappily for you, turn your back on tears and regrets instead. Don't allow bitterness or acrimony to take over where love left off. They are heavily self-destructive attitudes.

As the brilliant English novelist Evelyn Waugh once put it: 'The beastlier you are to others, the beastlier they become.' (He was born under Scorpio and so had the talent for hard-hitting comment!)

Agreed, it is hard to accept what you may regard as rejection or betrayal but never forget it takes two to tango and two to break a relationship. It is never solely his or her fault.

In the course of my work I have had a lot of experience with divorcing and divorced individuals. This experience has proved to me again and again the truth of Dr Erich Fromm's opinions in the book *The Art of Love*.

Undoubtedly, one of the greatest of the post-Freudian psychologists, Dr Fromm holds that without the capacity to love yourself you can neither love nor be loved. He does not mean of course that you should be selfish, self-centred or full of self-interest. Strange as it may seem at first glance, these qualities belong not to people who love themselves but to those who really hate themselves.

Loving yourself means accepting yourself for what you are, being proud of your good qualities and being willing to change the bad ones by positive, constructive thought and action.

Men and women who at heart hate themselves are destructive, unhappy, unloving and unloved. They constantly point the finger at others — tragically unaware that they are in fact, pointing the finger only at themselves. The divorce courts are full of such people. Don't become one of them if a broken relationship happens to you. Cut your losses. Accept your share of the blame. Then let bygones *be* bygones.

There's no future in the past!

Getting Through to Each Other

Last but not least, it's well to remember that renowned relationship wrecker — reluctance to speak your mind. Usually stemming from fear, shyness or inability to articulate, this attitude shows up all too often when Partner A can't, won't, or daren't tell Partner B what he/she likes or doesn't like, wants or doesn't want. You simply cannot assume your partner will get your message by some miraculous form of mental telepathy!

If you hate visiting your mother-in-law every Sunday, stop grinning and bearing it. Say so, tactfully, pleasantly. Then some workable compromise can be hammered out.

If you don't like some part of love-making your partner enjoys, discuss it — openly and willingly. Then the problem has some chance of being solved.

Otherwise, these unstated feelings of frustration will gradually crystallize into repressed anger and resentment that do far more harm to your relationship (and your health!) in the long run that even an outright fight about them at the outset could ever do.

Don't be surprised either at the melange of contradictory qualities you discover through the charts in yourself and your partner. Human beings *are* contradictory. That's what makes us interesting! Remember, too, nobody is thrust into close contact with another person for no reason at all. There is always a link between the two chart-wise or else their paths would never have converged in the first place.

Well, here we are at the end of our explorations into love and marriage, which *ought* to go together like a horse and carriage, but don't always. In a sense, we can now say that happiness in love is a bit like the old maxim about greatness. Some are born to be happy. (They're the 'naturals' but more the exception than the rule.) Some achieve happiness (after putting in a lot of heavy spade work on the job). Some have happiness thrust upon them (by a lover who cares long enough and deeply enough to haul them out of the shell of isolation).

Your charts will tell you where you belong in the above three. So now, it's over to you. And may all the pot-holes you strike along the rocky road be little ones!

BLANK FORMS FOR YOUR OWN ANALYSES

Male Partner Name........................... Female Partner Name...................

Birthdate.. Birthdate..................................

SOLAR COMPATIBILITY RATING TABLE

	His Personal Planets by Sign		Her Personal Planets by Sign
☉	(Ego)	☉	(Ego)
☽	(Emotions)	☽	(Emotions)
☿	(Mind)	☿	(Mind)
♀	(Affections)	♀	(Affections)
♂	(Sexuality)	♂	(Sexuality)

Male Partner Name........................... Female Partner Name...................

Birthdate.. Birthdate..................................

His Non-personal Planets by Sign		Her Non-personal Planets by Sign	
♃		♃	
♄		♄	
♅		♅	
♆		♆	
♇		♇	

	His	Elemental Stress Patterns	Hers	
Fire	=	Fire		=
Air	=	Air		=
Earth	=	Earth		=
Water	=	Water		=
Planetary Categories		**Planetary Categories**		
Cardinal signs		Cardinal signs		
Fixed signs		Fixed signs		
Mutable signs		Mutable signs		
Positive signs		Positive signs		
Negative signs		Negative signs		

Personality Profile and Summary of Natal Chart Indicators: Name

1. HEMISPHERE EMPHASIS:

............Planets above horizon; ....Planets below horizon

2. POSITIVITY/NEGATIVITY EMPHASIS:

............Points positive; ....Points Negative

3. REACTIONAL MODE EMPHASIS:

............Points Cardinal; ....Points Fixed; ....Points Mutable

4. ELEMENTAL EMPHASIS:

................Points Fire; ....Points Air

................Points Earth; .... Points Water

5. ANGULAR PLANETS STRESS: ....Angles stressed;
................1st ....4th ....7th 10th

6. NOTABLE CONFIGURATIONS:

7. POWER POINT CHARACTER PATTERN: Ascendant................
                                   Sun................
                                   Moon ....

8. LOVE AND SEX NATURE: Moon sign .... Moon house ....
                        Venus sign .... Venus house ....
                        Mars sign .... Mars house ....

9. SUCCESS DRIVES: Mercury sign .... Mercury house ....
                   Jupiter sign .... Jupiter house ....
                   Saturn sign .... Saturn house ....

10. MAJOR PLANETARY ASPECTS:
    SUN: .... Helpful; .... Difficult
    Should benefit from:

    Needs to watch:

    MOON: .... Helpful; .... Difficult
    Should benefit from:

    Needs to watch:

    MERCURY: .... Helpful; .... Difficult
    Should benefit from:

    Needs to watch:

VENUS: ....Helpful; ....Difficult

Should benefit from:

Needs to watch:

MARS: ....Helpful; ....Difficult

Should benefit from:

Needs to watch

CALCULATED COMPATIBILITY PROFILE

Male Partner Name:............................   **Female Partner name:**........................
Birthdate and time:............................   **Birthdate and time:**........................

CALCULATED COMPATIBILITY RATING TABLE

	His Personal Planets by Sign and Degree		Her Personal Planets by Sign and Degree
☉	(Ego)		(Ego)
☽	(Emotions)		(Emotions)
☿	(Mind)	☿	(Mind)
♀	(Affections)	♀	(Affections)
♂	(Sexuality)	♂	(Sexuality)

1. CHILDHOOD CONDITIONING:
    Male partner: Sign on 4th..
                     Planets in 4th..
    Female partner: Sign on 4th...
                     Planets in 4th..

    Remarks (male):

    Remarks (female):

2. MARITAL/PARTNERSHIP EXPECTATIONS:
    Male partner: Sign on 7th..
                     Planets in 7th..
    Female partner: Sign on 7th...
                     Planets in 7th..

    Remarks (male):

    Remarks (female):

3. ROMANTIC IDEALS — CONCERN WITH CHILDREN:
    Male partner: Sign on 5th..
                     Planets in 5th..
    Female partner: Sign on 5th...
                     Planets in 5th..

    Remarks (male):

    Remarks (female):

4. SOCIAL PROJECTION/COMMUNICATION:
    Male partner: Ascendant........................
                     Mercury sign........................
    Female partner: Ascendant........................
                     Mercury sign........................

    Remarks (male):

    Remarks (female):

5. CATEGORY COMPARISONS:
    Male partner: Elements........................
                     Polarities........................
                     Modes........................
    Female partner: Elements........................
                     Polarities........................
                     Modes........................

    Remarks (male):

    Remarks (female):

6. PLANETARY CROSS-REFERENCING:
    (Shown in Graphic Form on Rating Table)

    Direct:

    Remarks:

    Male Sun to female Sun:

    Male Moon to female Moon:

    Male Mercury to female Mercury:

Male Venus to female Venus:
Male Mars to female Mars:
Diagonal

(a) Compatible Aspects:

Remarks:

(b) Incompatible Aspects:

Summary of Findings from Chart Comparisons:

As per 1:

As per 2:

As per 3:

As per 4:

As per 5:

As per 6:

INDEX

By the same author . . .

HOW TO ASTRO-ANALYZE YOURSELF AND OTHERS

Making the most of yourself and your relationships

Astro-analysis is an exciting *new* way of finding out *what makes people 'tick'.* It uses *the best* of the old methods of astrology PLUS the very latest discoveries of modern psychology, and blends them together to come up with an absolutely fool-proof way of judging people and situations to enable *you* to profit by them.

- Find out what the people in your life are *really* like.
- *Know* who you can trust and who you can't.
- Be *successful* with the opposite sex.
- Become more *confident.*
- Be *happier* than you ever thought possible.

Now at last you can *take charge* of your life instead of just 'letting it happen'. This book is YOUR KEY TO A NEW, MORE SATISFYING LIFE!